NORTHERN IRELAND SCRAPBOOK

1. UDA recruiting poster.

2. IRA recruiting poster.

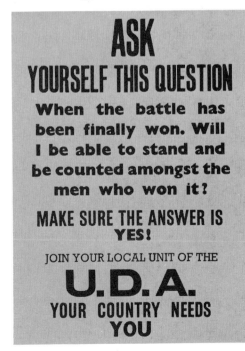

ASK
YOURSELF THIS QUESTION

When the battle has been finally won. Will I be able to stand and be counted amongst the men who won it?

MAKE SURE THE ANSWER IS YES!

JOIN YOUR LOCAL UNIT OF THE

U.D.A.
YOUR COUNTRY NEEDS YOU

IRISH REPUBLICAN ARMY

'Our aim .... to force a British withdrawal from Ireland and establish a democratic, socialist republic based on the Easter Proclamation'

3. Peace and tranquility: the Ulster countryside near the Mountains of Mourne (Northern Ireland Tourist Board)

Northern Ireland Scrapbook

John Chartres
Bert Henshaw
Michael Dewar

ARMS AND ARMOUR PRESS
London   New York   Sydney

4. Londonderry, April 1969. Tensions build.

Contents

First published in Great Britain in 1986 by Arms and Armour Press Limited, 2-6 Hampstead High Street, London NW3 1QQ.

Distributed in the USA by Sterling Publishing Co. Inc., 2 Park Avenue, New York, NY 10016.

Distributed in Australia by Capricorn Link (Australia) Pty. Ltd., P.O. Box 665, Lane Cove, New South Wales 2066, Australia.

British Library Cataloguing in Publication Data:
Chartres, John   Northern Ireland scrapbook
1. Northern Ireland – History – 1969–   I. Title   II. Dewar, Michael   III. Henshaw, Bert
941.60824   DA990.U46

ISBN 0-85368-870-2 (cased)   ISBN 0-85368-896-6 (paperback)

Jacket illustrations: Front cover main illustration shows rioting in the Bogside area of Londonderry; notice man with catapult on the right (Syndication International); and (inset) the clearing up after a night of rioting (Henshaw Collection). Back cover (cased edition only) shows fishing on Lough Erne (Northern Ireland Tourist Board); and (inset) an ugly incident in central Belfast involving The Royal Highland Fusiliers (The *Daily Mirror*).

The illustrations in this book have been collected from many sources, and vary in quality owing to the variety of circumstances under which they were taken and preserved. As a result, certain of the illustrations are not of the standard to be expected from the best of today's equipment, materials and techniques. They are nevertheless included for their inherent information value, to provide an authentic visual coverage of the subject.

Designed by David Gibbons; edited by Michael Boxall; typeset by Typesetters (Birmingham) Ltd., Smethwick, West Midlands; camerawork by Anglia Repro Ltd., Rayleigh; printed and bound in Great Britain by The Bath Press Limited.

TROOPS OCCUPY LONDONDERRY: 4,000 MORE ON WAY

Reinforcements From England — City Without Gas and in Peril of Famine.

DISTRICTS ISOLATED BY RAIL TROUBLE.

In consequence of the intervention of the troops, fighting in Londonderry had ceased yesterday, and the situation was much easier.

Many shops reopened, and sandbags were being removed from the streets.
The casualties are officially given as seventeen dead, twenty-nine wounded.
Fears of famine and the failure of the gas supply led to an assurance from the Government that the military authorities are taking all possible steps to restore order.
Various battalions are under orders to leave England for Ireland, and 4,000 additional troops are expected in Londonderry, increasing the garrison to 5,000 men.

Meanwhile, the refusal of railwaymen to transport forces of the Crown or to carry munitions is spreading, and parts of South-West Ireland are now isolated by the stoppage of trains.

FIGHTING QUELLED BY MACHINE GUNS.

Troops Rescue Women and Children Behind Barrage.

"PEACEFUL" LAST NIGHT.

Late on Wednesday night the troops in Londonderry opened a fire with machine guns, with the salutary effect that the rioting and factional fighting practically ceased.

The Derry situation, says an official report, was much easier yesterday. There was very little firing after midnight.

A military party bringing provisions to the gasworks was heavily fired at. The military returned the fire with their machine guns.

The military started removing sandbags yesterday morning. The General Officer Commanding, Belfast, has arrived in Derry, concludes the official statement.

At 8 a.m. a barber named Robert M'Loughlin was shot dead as he was entering a relative's house in Bishop-street. Mrs. Mills, wife of an ex-soldier, was shot through the heart in Ferguson's lane.

The nuns of Nazareth House, which faces St. Columb's College, informed the police that an eight-year-old girl named Carroll was killed in the institution by shots fired outside.

Apart from these incidents, everything was quiet in Derry. Some of the shops were opening, and people were moving about again.

"NO TRUCE!"

Nurse McCrossan, of Strabane, who tended wounded on the streets under heavy fire, received orders at midnight to leave her house in Abercorn-road, and shortly afterwards bullets rained through the windows of her bedroom.

She had a narrow escape, and was escorted from Abercorn-road to safe quarters under heavy fire.

One man was shot by her side near Carlisle Bridge.

Exciting scenes were witnessed when the military attempted to get a number of Protestants out of Barrack street.

An armoured car, supported by infantry with Lewis guns, made the attack.

An officer asked for safe conduct to get the refugees across, but was answered: "No truce. We have the stuff. Carry on."

The soldiers then set up a machine gun barrage, and behind this about fifty refugees, mainly women and children, succeeded in getting across to safety.

17 KILLED, 29 WOUNDED.

An official police statement gives the following return of casualties: Saturday, 5 killed, 10 wounded; Monday, 2 killed, 4 wounded; Tuesday, 3 killed, 1 wounded; Wednesday, 3 killed, 14 wounded; Thursday, 4 dead.

A man named McKinney, of Cross-street, who was shot on Wednesday morning, died yesterday in hospital. Patrick Mallett, Deanery street, wounded in the abdomen; Peter Campbell, the young Dungiven boy who was shot in the head while crossing the river also died yesterday.

A message despatched from Londonderry at 11.10 last night states that the position is absolutely peaceful.

HOW IT BEGAN.

Sinn Fein Anxious for First Blow Before "Derry Walls" Festival.

How all the trouble in Derry began is a question few in England could answer.

Deep-rooted bad feeling there has been for generations, as the population is about equally divided between Protestant and Catholic—Unionist, Nationalist and Sinn Fein.

There is no more exciting slogan in all Ulster than "Derry walls and no surrender."

The Orangemen, who have their young hot-bloods well organised, lead them in procession annually round the walls of the city, and the time for the observance of this rite is drawing near.

The Sinn Fein party were anxious to get their blow in first, and the present embittered state of the city is the result.

NEW ARMY OF 4,000 MEN SENT TO CITY'S AID.

Battalions Under Orders to Leave Aldershot.

FOOD SUPPLIES FAILING.

Sir Nevil Macready called at 10, Downing-street yesterday morning and had a further conference with the Prime Minister, who subsequently presided at a Cabinet meeting, at which there was a full attendance of Ministers.

"Food supplies are running out and the gas supply is almost exhausted. The situation is desperate and becoming worse hourly."

This urgent telegram was dispatched to the Irish Office by the magistrates of Derry.

Parts of the city are in a serious plight for food, no bread being baked, and the gas supply ceased at four o'clock yesterday morning.

The telegram added:—

More lives lost last night. Magistrates request reply and assurance from Government of immediate action to allay panic among citizens.

"ALL POSSIBLE STEPS."

The Irish Office dispatched the following reply:—

General Carter Campbell is taking, with approval of the Government, all possible steps to remedy present situation.

Military authorities on the spot have been instructed to keep magistrates informed of actions taken.

The Attorney-General for Ireland stated in the Commons yesterday that the military authorities were in command of the city, and that a curfew regulation had been applied and would remain in force until further notice.

It is stated that the force of troops in Derry is to be augmented, and that an additional 4,000 men are on their way to the city. This will bring the total garrison to 5,000.

The 1st Battalion of the Queen's Regiment, now at Aldershot, have received orders to move to Ireland within the next five days.

Other battalions in the command are preparing to move at short notice.

RAILWAY PARALYSIS.

Deadlock Spreading—Parts of South-West Ireland Isolated.

Messages received at the Irish Office, London, yesterday indicate that the Irish railway deadlock is spreading.

No trains have left Limerick on any branch, and the police are remaining in the trains protected by other police.

About thirty police, with baggage, arrived at the Limerick railway terminus yesterday, but the engine drivers refused to carry them.

Three trains to Dublin were held up, and some thirty drivers and guards were suspended.

Meetings of the Belfast branches, N.U.R., yesterday passed resolutions pledging support to the Government, and offering to handle any munitions that may pass through their hands, and to carry all troops.

Another P.C. Shot.—News has been received in Omagh that Constable Michael Horan, of the Tyrone Police Force, has been shot dead in County Tipperary while on temporary duty.

A WATER SCHEME TO SPEND MONEY.

A National Water Commission, composed of salaried members, and with absolute control over all the water resources of the country, is recommended in the report, just issued, of the special Board of Trade Committee on the industrial possibilities of the water power resources of the United Kingdom.

GRAFTED SHEEP'S NERVE ON ARM.

"I have grafted a nerve from a newly killed sheep on the arm of an officer who had two inches of the limb blown away, and he made a complete recovery," said Sir Charles Balance, lecturing in London yesterday to the Incorporated Society of Trained Masseurs.

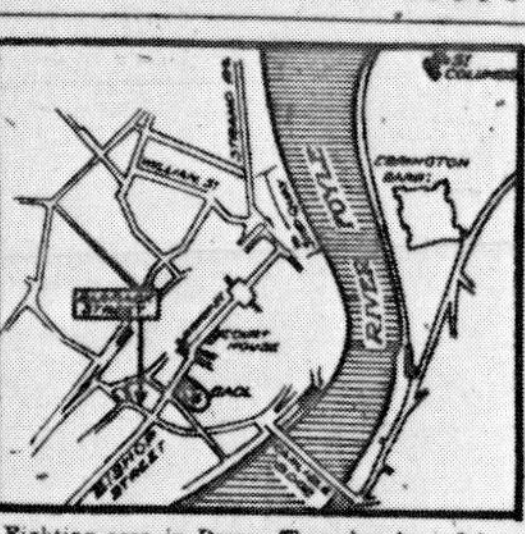

Fighting area in Derry: There has been firing from St. Columbs' grounds, in Barrack-street, and in Bishops-street.

FIRST GREEK VICTORIES IN THE NEW WAR.

Advance in Smyrna—Rebel Town Captured.

BRITISH SHIPS BUSY.

Turkish rebels at Ismid and other places were in full retreat yesterday, British naval bombardments and the commencement of Greek Army attacks having inflicted severe punishment on them.

The Greek offensive against Mustapha Kemal has begun victoriously, reports Reuter from Paris. The enemy, concentrated in the neighbourhood of Akhissar (north-east of Smyrna), was compelled to fall back in disorder, and Akhissar was occupied.

The Greek Legation in London last night described the advance as progressing favourably towards the north. Attacks have commenced on Salihoi and Alacher.

Athens reports that thousands of Greeks are flocking to the colours.

A Constantinople Exchange message received yesterday stated that the Nationalist troops con-

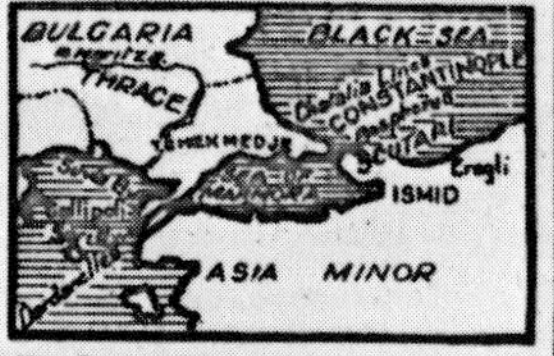

Map Showing Tchekmedje, where some of the Kemalists landed.

centrated at Sabandja were withdrawing, the British bombardment having resulted in a number of killed in their ranks.

The Kemalists are working feverishly on the construction of defence works on their lines, which are constantly widening. According to recent reports, the Kemalists have occupied the Greek town of Daridja.

Our warships shelled rebels from a distance of eight miles. A factory six miles north of Ismid used by the Nationalists as headquarters was demolished by our 15in. shells.

The British are maintaining a strong bombardment on the Ismid front. Mustapha Kemal's forces have retreated in the Bouyouk area in disorder. The first detachments of the Indian forces are installed on the heights around Bostanlik.

With a view to clearing up the position in Thrace, a considerable Greek force is being sent to Smyrna and Thrace in order to crush Jafer Tayar as a preliminary to the operations in Asia Minor.

Some of the Kemalists landed at Tchekmedje, on the European coast of the Sea of Marmora. This is regarded as an isolated attempt by the rebels to create trouble on the European coast.

The whole of the British Mediterranean Fleet and the First Battle Squadron are concentrated in the Marmora Sea and the Black Sea.

"THE GARDEN OF ALLAH."

Desert Drama of Passion at Drury Lane Theatre.

A dramatic version of Mr. Robert Hichens' book, "The Garden of Allah," was produced at Drury Lane last night. Like all Mr. Hichens' work—except his literary farces, which were extremely amusing—the atmosphere of the play is coloured with a certain hectic passion. But the story of the play, like the story of the book, is full of human interest. Mr. Hichens, as is his custom, has framed his version of the story in the background of the desert. As our Victorian fathers would say, the scenery is "simply stunning"; at any rate, it is in the best traditions of "old Drury." The acting of Mr. Basil Gill, Mr. Godfrey Tearle, and Miss Madge Titheradge was everything that a popular producer of popular plays could have wished.

MINISTER DEFENDS SPENDING SCHEMES.

Sir E. Geddes Puts Onus on Commons.

DEBATE SURPRISE.

Rule That Stopped Unfolding of New Policy.

There was a surprise in the Commons debate yesterday on the Vote for £848,042 for salaries and expenses of the Ministry of Transport. After Sir Eric Geddes had defended the Ministry for about two hours and was about to unfold the new policy of the department, it was discovered that this could not be disclosed in "Committee of Supply"!

So the proposals will now be revealed in a White Paper.

At the outset Sir Eric said a campaign of misrepresentation had been carried on as to the expenditure of the Ministry of Transport, and he had been accused of squandering the country's money.

He emphasised that the Select Committee on Expenditure had approved of everything that had been spent, and recommended further expenditure. All the Committee had said was that certain expenditure was not necessary this year.

As to the Ministry having been conceived on a grandiose scale, he reminded them that the House decided to set up the Ministry on the present scale after a division in which [illegible] voted for it and none against.

"A DUD SHELL, THAT!"

Salaries of the officials were not exorbitantly high, and the gentlemen who occupied these temporary posts had accepted them at great personal sacrifice to themselves.

He had succeeded in getting a pooling agreement on London railways cancelled at a saving to the country of £1,000,000.

Mr. Charles Palmer: We have lost a million and a half over a bad agreement.

Sir Eric Geddes: I have saved a million which would have been spent this year.

Dr. Murray: It is a "dud" shell, that!

If the Ministry had been a ruthless, wasteful Department, they would have appointed all the men provided for in the Estimates, but they did not do so, and that was called waste. The Press he left to themselves, but the House was always fair, and he left his case with them.

NO RAIL NATIONALISATION.

Turning to the future policy in regard to railways, the Minister argued that the present position was not the outcome of Government control, but of the general economic situation. Something must be done before the railways were handed back in the interests of the community and of the railway shareholders, who must be treated fairly and reasonably.

On the first alternative—national ownership—all the evidence went to show that State management was costly, that it lacked initiative and became "red tape."

Therefore the Cabinet, after full consideration, had decided not to recommend national ownership.

There was no reason for this enormous expenditure, Mr. Asquith contended. The Ministry included thirty officials, whose salaries amounted to £54,000, and five of them were described as "director-generals," of whose functions—potential or prospective—there was absolutely no explanation.

"An attack, not on the Estimates, but on the Ministry itself," was Mr. Bonar Law's summary of Mr. Asquith's speech. They were dealing with an absolutely unique situation, involving the superintendence of the expenditure of vast sums of money.

THAT UNDERGROUND AGREEMENT.

Sir Donald Maclean later said he suspected the consideration for the cancellation of that Underground agreement was to be found in the Bill for the increase of fares on the Underground Railway. (Cheers.)

Sir Eric Geddes said the agreement would be cancelled as from the date when the increased fares came into operation—(ironical Opposition cheers)—and quite properly so, because the wage bill expenses of the railway had increased.

Lord Ashfield had acted throughout as an honourable business man, and any suggestion to the contrary was untrue.

Mr. Arthur Neal said that, in response to the general desire of the House, the Government would give next Thursday for the further discussion of the vote. Progress was reported.

NEW ORDERS TO GERMANY.

Law Against Conscription and No Building Yet of Aircraft.

The *Journal* gives details of the Notes presented yesterday to Germany.

The first Note recalls that the reduction of the strength of the German Army to 100,000 men must be effected before July 10.

The second Note, drawn up by Marshal Foch and Sir Henry Wilson, demands that a law be passed abolishing conscription.—Reuter.

The Allies Brussels Conference takes place on July 2, and the Spa Conference with the Germans on July 6. Herr von Mayer is to be German Ambassador in Paris.

Introduction

This book is no more, and no less, than its title implies. It is a 'scrapbook'. At the risk of taking a negative line in its first words, I should say what it is *not*.

It is not yet another 'History of the Ulster Troubles 1968–1986'. There has been an abundant supply of such works over many years. It does not attempt to preach, to apportion blame, nor to suggest what the author might have done had he been a politician, a policeman or a general at the time. There has been a plentitude of that sort of book.

It *does* set out to show through the medium of the camera lens the sort of lives the residents of Northern Ireland have lived during the past twenty years. By 'residents' I include 'temporary residents' – that is the tens of thousands of British soldiers who have done tours of duty in Ulster since the momentous day of 14 August 1969.

The whole idea of this 'scrapbook' arose when Lieutenant-Colonel Michael Dewar of The Royal Green Jackets and Corporal Bert Henshaw of the same regiment suggested to the publishers that the latter's collection of pictures relating to the Northern Ireland problem could be of public interest. Corporal Henshaw, aged 40, with six tours in Northern Ireland under his belt, had decided at a fairly early stage of his military career upon the extra-curricular activity of building up a collection of photographs and other memorabilia.

When invited to be the compiler of his collection, I stipulated that it must be supplemented by pictures of events he had not been able to record – especially those of the 'formative years' of the Ulster problem before British troops entered the arena in August 1969. I also stipulated that the work must include illustrations of the normality of life, indeed the enjoyment of it, which has always gone on in Ulster even during the worst periods. This is something that has not always been appreciated by the outside world. For additional pictures I am especially indebted to friends on the staff of the *Daily Mirror* in Manchester and to that paper's management; to the Northern Ireland Tourist Board; to other Northern Ireland Government agencies and, perhaps remotely, to a number of publishing orgnizations in the Republic of Ireland.

5. The beginning of the current 'Ulster Troubles' is often dated from the appearance of British soldiers on the streets of Londonderry at 5 p.m. on 14 August 1969. Something of the sort had of course happened before as shown by this reproduction of the main news page of the *Daily Mirror* dated 25 June 1920.

In my own days as a British national newspaper reporter working in Northern Ireland during the formative years between 1969 and 1971, we used to parody some immortal Abraham Lincoln words by saying: 'We're lucky to please many of the people any of the time.' That, I fear, may still apply to anyone writing about the Northern Ireland tragedy. There is also a trite saying: 'The camera cannot lie.' This may, perhaps, be so; but the selection of the pictures that the camera takes can create a false impression, as every propagandist knows. As the compiler I can only plead I have done my best in selecting pictures that illustrate the lives the ordinary people of Northern Ireland have led. If bias is detected, as it surely will be, then it will probably be a bias against those who seek to achieve political objectives at the expense of the lives, the health and the happiness of innocent people. For that bias I make no apology.

The part played by newspapermen and others from radio and television organizations (nowadays lumped under the horrid word 'media') ought to be understood in reasonable terms and in the context of this book. It is sometimes overlooked that one of the contributory factors to the lack of understanding of the seriousness of the Ulster problem in the early 1960s in Westminster and Whitehall was that under the general construction of newspaper publishing the Irish editions of most national newspapers were produced in Manchester offices, rather than in London. This system, which still pertains, was always related to the 'catching of a boat' from Liverpool to deliver the papers in Ireland next morning.

The practice resulted in much well-informed news about Ireland being published only in the Irish editions of such papers as the *Daily Express, Daily Mail* and *Daily Mirror*. Once these editions had been produced, northern editors and chief sub-editors then cleared the Irish news out in order to make room for stories of import to areas such as Northumberland, Yorkshire, Merseyside and Manchester. An even smaller proportion of the news gleaned by expert journalists in Ireland ever found its way into the London editions, which were those read in the corridors of power at Westminster and Whitehall. Many superb photographs, some reproduced in this book, never caught the eyes of such people as Harold Wilson, James Callaghan or Edward Heath, at least until it was too late.

As a senior staff correspondent of *The Times*, based in Manchester and with a special interest in Northern Ireland affairs, I was seldom encouraged to spend more time in the

Province than strictly necessary. Apart from anything else, the aeroplane or ship fares were costly, not to mention the accommodation bills at the Grand Central or the Royal Avenue, not to mention the 'entertainment' expenditure incurred in talking to people in the pubs and clubs of the Falls and Shankill Roads. It finally fell to two British Sunday newspapers, The Observer and The Sunday Times to bring the dangers of the Ulster situation to the public eye in 1968, with Mary Holland of the former paper and the late David Holden of the latter plus its 'Insight' team really

setting the lead. After the importance of their stories struck home on the rest of what was loosely called 'Fleet Street' in those days, many more reporters like myself were encouraged to spend more time and money in Ulster.

Since this is essentially a picture book, the part played by television in the conflict ought to be mentioned. It is an important subject, perhaps deserving a book to itself. In the early days, television crews might have ben guilty of encouraging violence by their very presence and the desire of rioters and others to 'play to the camera.'

▲6 ▼7

▼8

6. British troops on the streets of Belfast in 1922.
7. British troops on the streets of Belfast (corner of North Street and Upper Library Street) in 1922.
8. Members of a C Specials police patrol in Albert Bridge Road, Belfast in 1922.

However certain ground rules were established at a fairly early stage and these were followed by both BBC and ITN crews. Unfortunately these rules were often broken by incoming crews from other nations, perhaps exacerbating potential riot situations. Little, if anything, has ever been put on paper about ground rules affecting television crews working in Northern Ireland, but most teams conform, if only for their own safety (which is, in fact, usually a minor consideration so far as they are concerned).

Many of the newspaper pictures in this book are attributed by name to the photographers who took them. Much credit must always go to the still photographers for the recording of the whole of the Ulster tragedy; they have always been more exposed to counter-violence than reporters, since their cameras appear as visible objects while a reporter's notebook or, indeed, personal memory can be concealed. I would like to pay personal tribute to the work, not only of those mentioned in the picture captions, but also to such 'resident photographers' as John Walters of the *Daily Mail*, Robert Renton of the *Daily Express*, Trevor McBride of *The Daily Mirror* and a great many unnamed photographers from regional and local newspapers, especially those on the staff of that superb newspaper, the *Belfast Telegraph*, which has 'soldiered on notwithstanding'.

Many of the photographs in the Henshaw Collection are the work of British Army photographers. This military trade was first recognized in the Second World War, with superb photographic work being carried out by young sergeants during the Battle of Alamein and elsewhere. For some reason, Army photographers are usually rated as sergeants, and are normally members of the Royal Army Ordnance Corps, a curious arrangement, since all civilian reporters and photographers are automatically given officer status when visiting any sort of service establishment. The main role of the sergeant photographers of the RAOC was in the field of publicity and recruiting until the Northern Ireland conflict broke out. By then, photography in the British Army had extended to the point where a battalion or equivalent formation would have its own skilled photographer. The Northern Ireland conflict imposed many more demands on photography – in particular the obtaining of 'mug-shots' of suspects to be woven into the Intelligence network. At one stage it seemed to outside viewers that more soldiers were carrying Leicas than carrying guns. Many of the pictures labelled as part of the Henshaw Collection should be regarded as a tribute to the photographers of the British Army. Obviously their work is of importance, not only in the Intelligence field, but also in the field of training young soldiers about to undertake their first tour of duty in Northern Ireland.

In any overview of the Northern Ireland situation, which this book really sets out to be, it should never be forgotten that normal life has gone on. For that reason a number of pictures labelled 'meanwhile' have deliberately been interspersed. In Northern Ireland work has continued; people have met, fallen in love and married; children have been born; crops have been sown and tilled. Young people have been taught in schools and universities – indeed, many young people from outside the Province have been very well taught in two universities, and many advances of knowledge have been achieved in both of them without much public recognition because the attention of the media has always been directed towards The Troubles.

This book does not include a mass of statistics, but some figures are worth recording. The total population of Northern Ireland increased from 1,502,000 in 1968 to 1,578,500 in 1984. That figure should take into account an outward migration of about 63,000 people, some of whom may have left because of the troubles, but many of whom might have left anyway in the normal course of job-seeking from a relatively confined community. Someone wisely said that there are 'lies, damned lies, and statistics'; nevertheless, these figures indicate that not many Northern Ireland people 'ran away' from the troubles. Some did, of course, leave for very good reasons, and none of them should in any way be branded as cowards. Many have made notable contributions in other parts of the British Isles and indeed the world at large.

Long before the current phase of the troubles began Northern Ireland was a high-unemployment area within the United Kingdom – but so of course were such areas as Tyneside, Merseyside and West Cumbria. During the period 1968–85 the total numbers *employed* in Northern Ireland ranged from 587,200 to 524,294 with a 'low' of 462,200 recorded in 1984. There never has been anything to be complacent about in Northern Ireland unemployment or 'lack of employment' statistics. Some areas, such as the border town of Strabane, have clocked up national record unemployment percentages.

It is often a matter of some astonishment to outsiders that there is such a thing as a tourist industry in Northern Ireland. However, it most certainly exists; indeed, it prospers. Some 900,000 people choose to visit the Province every year for holidays, providing a revenue of about £80 million. Not all that many visitors are British (for understandable reasons), but people from all over the world see no reason why they should not enjoy the delights of such places as Lough Erne and the Antrim coast at very reasonable prices, especially if they are interested in fishing. Up to the time of writing, few, if any, holiday visitors have been molested. At a very early stage of the troubles, a shrewd and distinguished member of the Stormont Parliament declared that the chances of a visitor being injured were about equal to that of being knocked down by a camel in Royal Avenue.

The words and pictures that follow therefore constitute an attempt to record what life has been like in Northern Ireland over a period of some twenty years. The three contributors have endeavoured to make it a fair and balanced account. We may not have succeeded, but at least we have tried.

9. The arena: an aerial view of central Belfast. (Henshaw Collection)

The formative years, 1968–70

The years 1968 and 1969 are often regarded as the 'formative' ones of the current Ulster problem, but for several years past there had been many danger signs for those who had eyes to see.

In the early and mid 1960s protests became more and more vociferous against the many disadvantages suffered by the Roman Catholic minority in such fields as jobs and housing. On the Protestant side there were counter-resentments and fears over the 'bridge-building' activities of the then Prime Minister, Captain Terence O'Neill, particularly over revelations that he had met and talked to Sean Lemass, the Taoiseach of the Irish Republic. The Reverend Ian Paisley began to emerge as the leader and spokesman of the 'hard-line' Protestants.

When the Queen visited the Province in 1966 tension and security were at a high level and a piece of concrete was thrown at, and hit, the Royal car. (It later transpired that there was no real political motive behind this incident.)

In early 1968 a broad-based Civil Rights movement made its presence felt and resentment by the Catholics and others of liberal persuasion came to a boiling-point when a 19-year-old unmarried Protestant girl was allocated tenancy of a council bungalow in the village of Caledon while hundreds of Catholic families in the Dungannon Council area remained on waiting-lists.

The 'Caledon incident' was followed by a large Civil Rights demonstration in the market town of Dungannon on 24 August 1968. There was no serious violence on that occasion, but the original plan for a march to enter the Protestant territory of the town's Market Square led to threats of a 'counter-demonstration' – a phrase which was to dominate the Ulster scene for many sad years to come. Police halted the marchers at a barrier a quarter of a mile from the town centre and some 2,500 Civil Rights supporters were separated from about 1,500 potential counter-demonstrators.

The next event, perhaps the most significant of 'the formative years', occurred on 5 October 1968 when Civil Rights supporters arranged a march through the divided city of Londonderry. The planned route would have taken them through the predominantly Protestant Waterside district. Mr William Craig, then Home Secretary in the Northern Ireland government, decreed that this would be a provocative and therefore illegal act and ordered the Royal Ulster Constabulary to prevent it. The march was halted and a conflict followed in which police officers used batons on the more determined marchers who included a

Westminster Member of Parliament, Mr Gerry Fitt. In Northern Ireland terms there was nothing new about the use of police batons. The difference was that television crews were present and millions throughout the British Isles and indeed other parts of the world, saw the ugliness of it all and many were horrified.

A month later in Armagh there was a confrontation between Civil Rights marchers and a 'defence force' of more than 1,000 Protestants, but violence was averted by the shrewd tactics of a senior RUC officer. That event resulted in a prison sentence for the Rev. Ian Paisley and a further build-up of tension.

In December 1968 Mr Craig, the 'hard-line' Home Secretary, was sacked by Prime Minister O'Neill and the latter became branded as a traitor by Mr Paisley's supporters.

After a Christmas truce more troubles erupted in January 1969. A 'Long March', initiated by some well-meaning Queen's University students, resulted in ugly incidents in which demonstrators were ambushed and attacked by so-called 'defenders' at a pretty little place called Burntollet Bridge with the apparent tacit approval and support of a number of police officers.

This, and another extraordinary event in which a party of police officers 'invaded' the Catholic Bogside area of Londonderry, fuelled the mounting criticism of the RUC as a sectarian and poorly disciplined force. It was to take many months, indeed years, for the RUC's reputation to recover from this inept action.

In January 1969 too, there was an ugly clash in the border town of Newry. Again the occasion was a Civil Rights march, which as planned would have taken the demonstrators through a Protestant area. This time the RUC were the losers, perhaps through no fault of their own. They endeavoured to prevent a confrontation, but in the course of it all a number of their trucks ('tenders') were set on fire and thrown into the Newry Canal. The compiler's main memory of this occasion is that of a sincere young Civil Rights leader, jumping on to a lorry, and almost in tears crying out: 'This has nothing to do with Civil Rights. Come away from this horrible place.'

A general election for the Stormont Parliament took place in February 1969. In overall terms the Unionist majority was confirmed but there were danger signs, not least being the result in the Bannside constituency where the Revd. Ian Paisley came a close second to the Prime Minister, Captain Terence O'Neill, with the People's Democracy candidate, Michael Farrell (representing the Catholic and other minority groups), a respectable third. Captain O'Neill (later Lord O'Neill of the Maine) resigned a few months later.

In March 1969 some curious events occurred. They took the form of explosions at power-stations and other public utility sites, which on the face of it were blamed on Irish Republicans, perhaps 'the IRA' — although such an organization did not really exist at that time. They all turned out to be a sort of 'double-take' job by extreme Protestants, but an important outcome was that some British troops, from units normally based in Northern Ireland for training purposes, were put on guard duty at certain public installations, especially at the colourfully named 'Silent Valley' reservoir in the foothills of the Mountains of Mourne. The British Army was again actively into the business of maintaining law and order in Ireland and it was never to look back.

In April 1969 Captain O'Neill resigned and was succeeded as Prime Minister by Major James Chichester-Clark, an amiable landowner, rather more acceptable to the Protestant majority than O'Neill, who by now had been labelled 'traitor'.

Peace of a kind followed until early August 1969 when fierce rioting broke out in the centre of Belfast around the Unity Walk flats, mainly occupied by Catholics but situated at the end of the Protestant Shankill Road stronghold. This often forgotten episode was triggered off by a rumour that a Young Unionists' march had been attacked by young Catholics. Very ugly scenes indeed transpired with Shankill Road Protestants attempting to storm the Unity Walk flats and indeed to set them on fire with petrol bombs. The RUC policemen involved displayed much gallantry and proved that they, at least, were NOT sectarian since they fought hard for several days to protect the Unity Walk residents. The rioting spread to other areas of Belfast and at one stage British troops from 2nd Battalion, The Queen's Regiment were put on stand-by. A number of officers and senior NCOs in plain clothes, were present as observers,

10. Members of the B Special Constabulary at a road-block near Ballycastle, Co. Antrim in 1932.
11. A wrecked Ulster Transport Authority bus after an attack in 1961.

knowing that the time could not be far off when they would be called upon. A full Company from this unit did in fact mount its vehicles and stood by on the outskirts of the city.

The next 'watershed' in the Ulster saga, the Bogside Riot episode in Londonderry in the middle of August 1969, was entirely predictable, at least to observers on the spot such as this compiler. The annual 'Apprentice Boys' March', a great demonstration of Protestant ascendancy was set to take place in Londonderry against mounting tension in this city and elsewhere, and Major Chichester-Clark, having listened to much advice, decided that it should be allowed to take place. The inevitable occurred. The Bogside residents felt that they were being taunted by the bands, the drums and the banners of the marching Protestants, not to mention the throwing of pennies from the high walls of the Protestant section of the city. Other ambitions and aspirations were fermenting in the Bogside.

This compiler has a clear and photographic memory of the 'first missile' – it was a marble, projected by a catpult, which missed the Protestant marchers but struck the glass roof of the public lavatories near the corner of William Street and the main square of Londonderry – which from now on will be referred to as 'Derry'. Nothing was going to be the same again. I remember a distinguished colleague, Mr Harry Jackson of *The Guardian*, and I saying to each other: 'We're Off'.

The marble was followed by bricks and later by petrol bombs. The police saw as their task the prevention of the Bogside residents from entering the city centre. The Bogside residents saw as their task the prevention of the police from entering their territory. Barricades were erected, and for several days and nights the fighting continued, bricks and petrol bombs on one side, policemen with the bricks they could pick up, on the other. Then the police were given authority to use CS gas. This didn't help much – as was later proved, this is a singularly useless 'weapon' for riot control.

After three days the police were showing signs of exhaustion, and there was an apparent risk that the Bogsiders might break out and ravage the city. Urgent discussions went on between the Stormont and Westminster governments, some members of the latter organization at last being made aware that serious things were really happening in Northern Ireland.

On 14 August 1969 (a date to be remembered) the mobilization of the 'B' Specials was authorized, and some were deployed in Derry. A little later that day the British Prime Minister, Mr Harold Wilson and his Home Secretary, Mr James Callaghan, authorized 'Military Aid', and at 5 p.m. troops of 1st Battalion, The Prince of Wales's Own Regiment of Yorkshire, moved into the centre of Derry, having been alerted several days previously. This compiler was present in the main square of Derry when the first British troops arrived. There was what can only be described as a relaxed hush and a corporate sigh of relief. The arrival of the soldiers, most of them looking extra-

ordinarily young, fit and pink, and the 'far-back' tones of a Major inviting an Inspector of the B Specials to march his men away in good order, was followed by a parley through a fire-engine's loud-hailers by Mr Stanley Orme, MP, from the Bogside side of the barricades gave us the impression that it was all over. How wrong we all were.

That same night even worse violence broke out in the Falls Road area of Belfast, this time involving the use of firearms. Some units of the RUC, mounted in light armoured vehicles, over-reacted to a real or imagined threat and fired automatic weapons.

On the night of 14/15 August ten people were killed, including a British soldier on leave at his home in the Divis Street flats; 145 civilians and four policemen were wounded. Again it fell to the Army to restore the situation and a few days later troop reinforcements were flown in.

An uneasy peace, sometimes called the British Army's 'honeymoon period', followed. The Catholic populations of the Falls Road and other residential districts of Belfast barricaded themselves in, but displayed confidence in the British troops as peacemakers in contrast to their suspicion and fear of the RUC.

A package of social and legal reforms, most of it instigated from Westminster was put into effect. It included the disbandment of the RUC's B Specials and their eventual substitution by a locally recruited Ulster Defence Regiment under British Army high command control. The latter part of the package led to a serious outbreak of violence, and the use of firearms, in the Protestant Shankill Road area in October 1969. For the first time in what can be dubbed 'the current phase' of Irish troubles, British soldiers had to open fire on the streets.

In the background, however, as Christmas 1969 approached, other significant events were taking place. The most significant of all was the formation of an organization known as the Provisional IRA.

Towards the end of the year a child was wounded in the Falls Road area of Belfast while playing with a pistol he had found in his home. The policemen who were called to help stumbled upon a cache of 13,000 rounds of 9mm ammunition in the child's bedroom. That incident received only scant attention in the newspapers, but to many it was a frightening indicator of what was to come.

12. Tension mounting in the mid 1960s. A demonstration in front of a bus in the middle of Belfast on 26 July 1966. (*Daily Mirror*)

13. An example of the pictures that appeared on television screens throughout the British Isles, and indeed the world, showing the ugliness of a confrontation between demonstrators and policemen. This picture shows Civil Rights demonstrators in conflict with RUC policemen during the course of what had been declared an 'illegal demonstration and march', in Londonderry on 5 October 1968. This event, and the pictures like this, which were taken of it, were to change many facets of life in the United Kingdom, and even farther afield. (*Daily Mirror*)

14. Another instance of confrontation between Civil Rights demonstrators and the RUC in Londonderry on 5 October 1968. Happily, this seems to have been a sensible and non-violent confrontation. (*Daily Mirror*)

15. Confrontation between Civil Rights demonstrators and the RUC spreads south to the City of Belfast. An encounter on 5 November 1968 in the City centre. (Cyril Cain, *Daily Mirror*)

16. At one stage during the 'Troubles' it was thought that water cannon would be adequate weapons to deter rioters, but they never proved effective. Here is one in action in Londonderry in October 1968. A great many people are getting wet and a parked car is obviously getting a good wash. (*Daily Mirror*)

17. A picture taken during what was termed 'The Long March' – an effort initiated by a number of concerned students at Queen's University, Belfast, in support of the Civil Rights Movement of 1968/69.

It was alleged, and there is much photographic and verbal evidence in support, that the marchers were deliberately ambushed at Burntollet Bridge by 'Loyalist' opponents, and that many suffered injury while elements of the RUC at best only stood by, and perhaps even encouraged the ambushers.

18. Another picture of 'The Burntollet Ambush'. This is claimed to show 'attackers' wearing white armbands and RUC officers and Constables in close collaboration.

19. Meanwhile, people continued to enjoy the scenery and the beauty of Northern Ireland. A couple look at Lough Shannagh in the Mountains of Mourne. (Northern Ireland Tourist Board)

▲16 ▼17

▼18

19

20. An RUC 'tender' burning during riots at Newry in January 1969. Several other similar vehicles were burned and thrown into the canal running through the border city during an early 'rough night' in which the compiler was chased by a baton-bearing policeman, but managed to out-distance him through a combination of fear and adrenalin. (*Daily Mirror*)

▲22 ▼23

21. Another personal conflict between a young Londonderry man and policemen, the latter now equipped with riot shields and protective helmets. This was a typical incident following an incursion into the Roman Catholic Bogside area made in 1969 by an undisciplined group of RUC policemen. One of the many 'official inquiries' into the Ulster troubles resulted in the 'Cameron Report' which said of the RUC officers concerned that they had been 'guilty of misconduct, assault and battery, malicious damage to property and the use of provocative and sectarian slogans'. That deplorable episode has now been largely forgotten in the history of the Ulster Troubles, but it perhaps explains why conflicts such as this took place in April 1969. (*Daily Mirror*)

22. Tension mounted in the summer of 1969. A mill is set on fire in Londonderry during a conflict in July. (*Daily Mirror*)

23. A personal conflict in Londonderry between a Republican demonstrator and an RUC officer in July 1969. (*Daily Mirror*)

▼24

24. A scene that was to become familiar. A burnt-out bus used as a barricade during the riots in Belfast in early August 1969 which preceded the Londonderry 'Bogside Riots' and which nearly led to the introduction of troops on the streets. (*Daily Mirror*)

▲25   ▼27   ▲26

▼28

25. An early stage of the 'Bogside riots'. Police with helmets, shields and batons face Catholic rioters in William Street, Londonderry with the Rossville Street flats in the background. Shortly after this picture was taken (on 12 August) the RUC was authorized to use CS gas. (*Daily Mirror*)

26. Another scene in William Street, Londonderry on 12 August 1969. (*Daily Mirror*)

27. Fires were lighted. (*Daily Mirror*)

28. Fires were lighted. A bakery on fire in the centre of Londonderry on the night of 13/14 August. (*Daily Mirror*)

29. A petrol bomber in action from a rooftop in Londonderry during the Bogside Riots. (*Daily Mirror*)

30. A petrol bomb 'factory'. Note the 'operative' in the background, believed to be about seven years old. (*Daily Mirror*)

▲31 ▼32

▲33 ▼34

▼35

31. British troops are 'on the streets'. This young soldier, probably from 1st Battalion, The Prince of Wales's Own Regiment of Yorkshire, the first unit to be deployed, looks puzzled as he tries to help distressed people. His bayonet is fixed – a practice which was rapidly discontinued. (*Daily Mirror*)

32. British troops in a confrontation in Belfast in September 1969. They are dressed in their normal combat clothing of the time – standard steel helmets and waterproof capes. (*Daily Mirror*)

33. Reinforcements arrive. Troops of 1st Battalion, The Queen's Regiment disembarking from the Royal Fleet Auxiliary Logistic Support ship *Sir Tristram* at Londonderry on 19 August 1969. They were commanded by Lieutenant-Colonel Charles Millman, a colourful and warm-hearted officer who did his best to establish rapport between both communities in Londonderry during his tour of duty, but with only moderate success. (*Daily Mirror*)

34. An episode illustrating what the British Army at that stage hoped would be a 'Hearts and Minds' operation. A bride and bridegroom, who had married during the heat of the Bogside Riot period, are joined by soldiers – whose bayonets are no longer fixed. (*Daily Mirror*)

35. British troops helping to lower barricades in Belfast in early September 1969 – a period of hope. They are unarmed and wearing berets rather than steel helmets. Technical experts from the Royal Engineers can be detected among the infantrymen by their cap badges. (*Daily Mirror*)

36. Meanwhile. Much of life in Belfast went on as normal. A scene in Donegall Place, in 1969. (Northern Ireland Tourist Board)

37. Children and soldiers have always had a special fascination for one another. Lance-Corporal Kenneth Martin of 2nd Battalion, The Light Infactry, with 21-month-old Johnny Murphy 'somewhere in Belfast' in September 1969. Corporal Martin's own son was 21 months old at the time this picture wa taken. (*Daily Mirror*)

▲36 ▼37

▼38

38. Soldier with children, Belfast, September 1969. (*Daily Mirror*)

39. The British troops 'settle down to a long war'. Mr Denis Healey, then Secretary of State for Defence, visiting troops in their billets in Londonderry in September 1969. (*Daily Mirror*)

40. Early October 1969 and relationships remain relaxed between the population and the security forces. A Military Policeman (still able to wear his No. 2 Dress with white belt and red cap) and an RUC officer help an elderly lady with a problem in the Bogside area of Londonderry. (*Daily Mirror*)

▲**39**   ▼**40**

▲41 ▲42

▼44 ▲43

▼45

41. In October 1969 these British soldiers, an infantry Lance-Corporal and a Corporal of the Royal Military Police were able to patrol the Bogside area of Londonderry in No. 2 Dress without weapons or any form of protective clothing. This was a short-lived phase! (*Daily Mirror*)

42. Shorland armoured cars of the RUC patrolling a riot-strewn Belfast street in August 1969. (*Daily Mirror*)

43. B Specials of the RUC drawing pistols in August 1969 shortly before they were 'stood down' after the arrival of British troops on the streets of Ulster. (*Daily Mirror*)

44. Hard facts have to be faced. British troops, wearing gas masks as a protection against the possible launching of their own CS gas, rehearse in Belfast. The relaxed onlookers and their expressions of curiosity indicate that this picture was almost certainly taken during an exercise, in September 1969. (*Daily Mirror*)

45. But stresses and tensions were still building. A typical Belfast barricade in October 1969. (*Daily Mirror*)

▲46

▲47

▼49

48

46. Children made friends with soldiers. (*Daily Mirror*)
47. Children played with soldiers. (*Daily Mirror*)
48. Again – children played with soldiers. (*Daily Mirror*)
49. But children played at being rioters. (*Daily Mirror*)

▲50 ▼51

50. And in October 1969 the British Army had to deploy some of its heaviest armoured vehicles, Saracen personnel carriers, on the streets of Belfast to quell riots. (*Daily Mirror*)

51. In mid October 1969 serious violence erupted in the Unity Walk area of Belfast following the announcement that the RUC's B Specials were to be disbanded. A policeman, PC Victor Arbuckle, and two other civilians were killed. Fourteen soldiers, three policemen and twenty civilians were taken to hospital with gunshot wounds. The first shots were fired by the British Army in the current 'phase' of the Ulster troubles – 66 rounds. It was estimated that 1,000 rounds were fired *at* British soldiers by enraged Protestants from the Shankill Road area before authority was given to troops to reply in self-defence. (*Daily Mirror*)

52. Fighting around the Unity Walk flats. (*Daily Mirror*)

53. Nevertheless relations between troops and civilians remained good into 1970. (Henshaw Collection)

54. Meanwhile, the countryside of Northern Ireland looked as beautiful as ever to this little girl gazing over Glenariff in Co. Antrim. (Northern Ireland Tourist Board)

▼52   ▲53

54

The battle lines, 1970–2

The period up to Christmas 1969 has been described as the 'formative' one. The years of 1970, 1971 and 1972 were those in which the Security Forces, consisting of the British Regular Army, the RUC, and to an increasing extent, the Ulster Defence Regiment, finally became locked in battle with Republican extremist organizations; almost always with what had been labelled the 'Provisional Wing of the IRA' – though others were to appear on the sidelines.

Again, perhaps the most significant event at the end of 1969 and the beginning of 1970 was the formation of the 'Provisionals' as a result of many clandestine discussions both in Dublin and Belfast. Many of those who had participated in earlier IRA campaigns against the British were smarting under the taunt that 'IRA' stood for 'I Ran Away' (when the Catholic communities in Belfast came under fire from the RUC's armoured cars on the night of 14/15 August 1969).

The so-called 'Official' IRA had by then turned its political eyes leftwards, believing that the objective of a United Ireland could best be achieved by political activity only, perhaps supported by the forces of world-wide Marxism. There were those who thought otherwise; believing that the correct course was to fight with the bullet and the bomb, and their overt leader was Ruairi O'Bradaigh (anglicized into 'Rory O'Brady'). At an early stage of the conflict the Security Forces were apt to refer to their 'opposition' as 'Brady IRA' or in radio network

55. 'Winning the Hearts and Minds of the People'. In the centre the then Corporal Percy Roach of 1st Battalion, The Parachute Regiment with young friends from the Shankill Road area of Belfast. Corporal (later Company Sergeant-Major) Roach became a sort of 'Pied Piper' because of his own interest in, and rapport with, youngsters, especially on the Rugby field. (Henshaw Collection)

code jargon as 'Bravo-Type India Romeo Alpha'. (At about this time rioters without much political motivation were referred to on radio nets as 'Yobboes', and very young brick-throwers as 'Yoblets'. The British Army has always tried to maintain some humour in its radio parlance and it added 'Black Magic' as a reference to priests in its standard 'Appointments Code' which as every old soldier knows starts with the Commanding Officer being called 'Sunray'.)

During the winter of 1969–70 dedicated Republicans felt it necessary to do something about a situation in which British soldiers were being welcomed into Catholic communities in the North, given tea and buns on doorsteps; with Catholic girls going to discos arranged under the British Army policy of 'winning the hearts and minds of the people', which had worked well in places like Malaya and Borneo, and which, at the time, they honestly thought would work in Northern Ireland. A propaganda campaign was therefore the first activity conducted by the Provisionals, who at that stage did not have much in their hands in the way of lethal weapons. The campaign was fairly crude but none the less effective. Of course among some 20,000 British soldiers in the Province sufficient human errors were being made to provide ammunition for any propagandist – such as the kicking in of a door during an arms search with a totally innocent Catholic family

living behind it, and perhaps a bit of 'aggro' between a young soldier trying to become a policeman overnight and some Catholic lads out on a spree.

By early 1970 the IRA had virtually won its propaganda battle and, too late, the British Army tried to react to it, but sometimes in quite the wrong way and with some over-reactions which had deplorable results. By early 1970 the Catholic communities were 'polarized' against the British Army and there were no more cups of tea or buns for soldiers patrolling the Falls Road or thereabouts.

The main political events of 1970 were that in April the Rev. Ian Paisley won the Bannside seat in the Stormont Parliament and a few weeks later became a Westminster MP representing North Antrim.

On 21 August 1970, a new and most important political organization, the Social Democratic and Labour Party was formed in Northern Ireland. It absorbed most of the supporters of the old Nationalist Party, the National Democratic party and the Republican Labour Party. It stood for 'Civil Rights for All and Just Distribution of Wealth'. Its leader, and in a way its architect, was John Hume of Derry, a politician of extraordinary resolve and tenacity, to whom the world owes much.

On the military scene in early 1970 the British Army was having to re-adjust itself from its hoped-for 'Hearts and Minds' policy towards riot control and other unpalatable matters. On arrival in Ulster the Army's 'riot drill' dated back to the days of the Raj, with a white line being marked across a road and a banner displayed in the local language saying: 'Disperse or We Fire'. The next act in this drill was for the Officer in Charge to issue an order to a nominated marksman on the lines of: 'Ringleader wearing red turban second-from-the-left, One Round Fire to Kill'. That system had worked right up to the days of the troubles in Aden

56. A message of a kind seldom repeated after 1969.
57. During what was later dubbed as the British Army's 'honeymoon period' 1st Battalion, The Parachute Regiment built up special relationships with the population. Its Commanding Officer, the then Lieutenant-Colonel Michael Gray (later Lieutenant-General Sir Michael Gray), is towards the right of picture, talking to the Chief of the Defence Staff, Marshal of the Royal Air Force, Sir Charles Elworthy. On the extreme left is Lieutenant-General Sir Ian Freeland, Commander-in-Chief, Northern Ireland, when this picture was taken early in 1970.

56   57

and elsewhere east of Suez until the mid 1960s. It was NOT, however, really appropriate for the Northern Ireland situation. (One distinguished British Army officer is on record as saying that the main thing that form of riot drill taught was that one should NEVER go to a riot wearing a red turban.)

In early 1970, however, the Army units equipped themselves with riot shields, visored helmets and batons and evolved a system of 'snatch-squads'. They also practised using CS (Consolidated Smoke) gas, even though it ineffectiveness had been proved at Derry in August 1969.

In April 1970 the Provisional IRA showed its teeth with 29 explosions, mainly directed against such 'hard targets' as police stations, prison gates, post offices and British-owned airline offices. This campaign brought to the notice of the nation the skills of the ATOs (Ammunition Technical Officers) of the Royal Army Ordnance Corps, described in more detail later.

Just after Easter 1970 the Army became involved in trying to quieten serious rioting in the predominantly Catholic housing estate of Ballymurphy, triggered off by a typical 'Marching Day' confrontation. The Army units fired a lot of CS gas and some of the Ballymurphy residents threw a lot of petrol bombs. This led to the GOC of the time, Lieutenant-General Sir Ian Freeland, to declare that a 'persistent petrol bomber' could be regarded as a legitimate target for shooting by one of his soldiers.

In June 1970 the first serious gunfights occurred in Belfast, between elements of what were identified as IRA units and some militant, and armed, Protestants.

In the late summer of 1970 both Army and RUC patrols came under fire from such crude weapons as nail bombs (made of corrugated cardboard, with nails stuck in the corrugations and a stick of easily obtained quarry gelignite in the centre), occasionally from 1914–18 .45 Webley pistols or from 'tommy-guns' – see picture caption. There were many miraculous escapes, but in November 1970 the British Army's Commander Land Forces, the then Major-General Anthony Farrar-Hockley, proclaimed at a press conference: 'We are now geared up to face a prolonged terrorist campaign.'

The major political event of 1970, often overlooked in studies of the Ulster conflict, was the UK general election in June, in which the Conservatives took back control from Labour. The result meant that politicians such as James Callaghan, and indeed Harold Wilson, who had perhaps belatedly, shown understanding of, and sympathy with, the Ulster problem were ousted and replaced by representatives of a party which had traditionally never 'interfered' with the locally elected Unionist Stormont Parliament.

James Callaghan was replaced as Foreign Secretary by Reginald Maudling. On his first visit to Ulster the latter uttered what were to become immortal words. He said that what could be aimed at, and probably achieved, was 'an acceptable level of violence'. At the time he was 'laughed out of court', but many, many years later his words began to make sense, and indeed at the time of writing this book, still make *common sense*.

By the end of 1970 a total of 38 people had died as a direct result of the latest phase of 'Irish Troubles': 35 civilians, including twelve classified in Security Forces files as 'terrorists', and three policemen. Some early words uttered by the former Ulster Prime Minister, Captain Terence O'Neill, that it would only be a short step from the brick and the petrol bomb to the bullet and the high-explosive bomb, were being proved.

What can only be described as the 'dreadful' year of 1971 was heralded by the death of the first British soldier in February; followed by those of three young Scottish soldiers a month later and by that of a Parachute Regiment sergeant two months after that – see picture captions for details.

Major Chichester-Clark resigned the Ulster Premiership in March 1971 because he was dissatisfied with the Westminster Government's lack of understanding of the seriousness of the position and their unwillingness to back his requests for much tougher measures by the Security Forces, including the posting in of more troops. He was succeeded by Mr Brian Faulkner.

On 9 August 1971 Mr Faulkner, with the approval of Mr Maudling and of Mr Edward Heath, then Prime Minister, ordered 'Internment without Trial'. This was another date to be etched into the calendar of the Ulster conflict. Hindsight indicates that the internment operation, with its enormous consequences, was clumsily executed. Intelligence information was badly out of date, and many of the wrong people were locked up. The whole affair became a 'gift' to the Republican propagandists who made full use of the many understandable abuses, especially when evidence inevitably came to the surface that some very rough interrogation procedures had been used, coming close to the current definitions of 'torture'. Thirty people were killed in the violence which followed.

Some efforts at a political solution were made including Tripartite talks at Chequers involving Mr Heath, Mr Faulkner and Mr Jack Lynch, the Irish Premier, but they came to little.

The year of 1971 ended with an especially horrific bomb explosion in McGurk's Bar in Belfast in which fifteen people died. At first thought to have been an 'own goal' in Security Forces' terminology – i.e., an accidental explosion killing the terrorists who plant the bomb – the incident was proved, much later, to have been the work of 'Loyalist' extremists.

The 'fresh' fatalities for 1971 amounted to 174 – 43 British Regular soldiers, five members of the UDR, eleven policemen, 61 civilians, 52 others classified as 'IRA terrorists' and two classified as 'Loyalist terrorists'. That brought the total death-roll to more than 200, and the figures did NOT take into account the 'wounded' or 'injured'. As with so many casualty statistics the fate of those whose lives have been ruined for ever, for physical or psychological reasons, is not properly recorded in them.

The equally horrific year of 1972 opened in January with the 'Bloody Sunday' episode in Derry about which so much has been written. In this book perhaps it need only be recorded that thirteen civilians were killed by British soldiers. Whether any of those who lost their lives ought to be included in the 'terrorist' classification will remain an open question until the end of time. This compiler, having been present, but like everyone else, only able to see and observe at first hand certain parts of the melancholy affair, can only say, again with the easy facility of hindsight, that it need not have happened. Most journalists, however, used to recording disasters, will say about almost any tragedy, that it was brought about by a number of sins of *omission*, rather than by a single sin of *commission*. One could indeed say that about the whole of the Ulster tragedy.

Be that as it may, 'Bloody Sunday' was to polarize the whole conflict even more sharply. The divided cities of Derry and Belfast became even more divided and the battle lines between the Security Forces and the Catholic populations even more clearly drawn. Horror followed upon horror. The conflict was taken to the mainland with the bombing of The Parachute Regiment's barracks in Aldershot with seven innocent people killed.

On 4 March the Abercorn Restaurant in Belfast was blown up killing two girls and injuring many other people; and then came 'Bloody Friday' on which day (21 July) 22 bombs were exploded, nine people killed and nearly 150 injured in the city.

On 24 March 1972 the British Government announced Direct Rule in Northern Ireland. Inevitably, this had short- and long-term repercussions. In July 1972 the Army and the Police broke into what had become termed as 'No-Go' areas in Belfast and Derry – those parts of the cities in which the IRA rather than Her Majesty's Government virtually held the writ of law and order. This was called Operation 'Motorman' and involved for the first time the deployment of 'tanks' – actually these were AVREs (Armoured Vehicles, Royal Engineers) used in the bull-dozer role to clear barricades in Derry, and rapidly spirited away once the job had been done.

In November 1972 the IRA used a Soviet-designed RPG-7 rocket launcher against the Police Station in the charming little Border town of Belleek in Fermanagh, the scene of many a previous engagement and also the home of the much sought-after pottery bearing its name. That incident ushered in another phase of the conflict with the IRA clearly having access to quite sophisticated weapons on world-wide arms markets.

The 'fresh' casualty list for 1972 numbered 467 dead: 103 from the Regular British Army, 26 from the UDR, 17 from the RUC, 223 from the civilian population, 95 classified as 'Republican terrorists', three classified as 'Loyalist terrorists'. The end of the year brought the grand total of deaths to 667. The 'watershed figure' of 1,000 dead, which many had been laughed at for predicting three years earlier, was inexorably coming closer.

58. A Para and a young friend somewhere in Belfast, *circa* January 1970. (Henshaw Collection)
59. Paras and other young friends, somewhere in Belfast, *circa* January 1970. (Henshaw Collection)

60. Soldiers and civilians argue out a few points in a Catholic district of Belfast early in 1970. The soldiers carry rifles and gas masks but they see no reason to wear anything more protective on their heads than their regimental berets. (Henshaw Collection)

61. The 'honeymoon period' comes to an end. British troops facing rioters in Derry in March 1970. At this stage they have been equipped with crude shields; at least their leader has slightly more effective headgear than the standard steel helmet — either a paratrooper's helmet or perhaps a motor-cycle dispatch rider's 'crash-hat', retrieved from stores. (*Daily Mirror*)

62. A rather different relationship between soldiers and a child in the Bogside district of Derry in March 1970. The expression on the face of the Corporal on the right should be studied, however. Was this really a case of 'Army brutality' or were the soldiers helping, to get a little boy home to his Mum? (*Daily Mirror*)

63. Tension built up in 1970. 'Suspects' being searched by soldiers in the standard manner somewhere in Belfast. (Cyril Cain, *Daily Mirror*)

64. Tempers can be lost, and control can be lost during close confrontations between security forces and protesters. (A scene in Leeson Street, Belfast captured by Bill Kennedy of The *Daily Mirror*)

65. Meanwhile, people went on 'back-packing' in the Glens of Antrim. (Northern Ireland Tourist Board)

▲61 ▼62

▲63 ▼64

65

67

A BRITISH Army
sergeant who
gave his life to save
four people from a
terrorist bomb has
been awarded a post-
humous George Cross.

Two of those who
escaped the blast were
children.

They were shielded by
27 - year - old Sergeant
Michael Willets as the
explosion ripped through
Springfield-road police
station in Belfast.

The citation in the
London Gazette, says

66. The 'watershed' tragedy of the night of February 5/6 1971. Gunner Ronald Curtis, aged 19, lies dead on a pavement in Lepper Street, Belfast. He was the first of (to date) nearly 400 British Regular soldiers to be killed in action. His wife Joan, was pregnant. Gunner Curtis was almost untrained in the arts of street-fighting, being a trainee surveyor in a specialized Royal Artillery unit which had been drafted in to Belfast to act as infantry because of the shortage of troops at that time. He was struck by an almost spent round, from a burst of Thompson submachine-gun fire, which entered the shoulder gap in his flak jacket, struck his heart, but did not 'exit'. Consequently he shed no blood, and on his face there was no sign of pain. Those shown in the picture trying to comfort him did not realize that he was dead until the lighted cigarette placed in his mouth, failed to glow. The compiler is 'just out of frame'. He and the photographer were the only journalists present and neither slept at all that night. (Photograph by Robert Renton, then of The Daily Express Belfast staff, now Picture Editor of The Star.)

67. Another 'watershed' tragedy for the British Army. Sergeant Michael Willets of 3rd Battalion, The Parachute Regiment, a popular and familiar figure as his Commanding Officer's personal radio-operator, died trying to protect four civilians, two of them young children, when a terrorist bomb was brought into the combined RUC/Army Headquarters in Springfield Road on 25 May 1971. He was posthumously awarded the George Cross, but when his body was carried out of the debris after the explosion some women living in the area spat upon the stretcher. (*Daily Mirror*)

68,69 The ugliness of 'close-quarter' fighting between security forces and demonstrators. These two pictures were taken during a confrontation between demonstrators, many of them women, from a tobacco factory in the centre of Belfast, and soldiers of 1st Battalion, The Royal Highland Fusiliers. In studying these pictures it is perhaps important to remember that three young soldiers from this battalion had, a few weeks before, been abducted by young women, lured to a remote country lane and shot in the back of the head. This affray, which not only resulted in still pictures such as these, but also in a TV sequence, brought special distress to the Battalion's Commanding Officer, Lieutenant-Colonel David Anderson, a Roman Catholic, who had made exceptional efforts to establish rapport between his soldiers and both sections of the Ulster population. (William Kennedy, *Daily Mirror*)

▲**68** ▼**69**

70. Inevitably, by early summer 1971 the Army had to take a tougher line in its 'peace-keeping' operations. Suspects being searched in the Markets area of Belfast. (Henshaw Collection)

71. During the violence which inevitably followed internment on 9 August 1971 a young British soldier tries to help and comfort someone, somewhere. A study of their expressions may indicate that HE doesn't really know what it is all about nor does SHE. (*Daily Mirror*)

72. But in Derry young people and soldiers remained enemies. A British Army four-tonner burning after a clash over who knows what in July 1971. (*Daily Mirror*)

73. Security measures get tougher. A 'VCP' (Vehicle Check Point) in the Lower Falls Road, Belfast in July 1971. (Henshaw Collection)

▲70 ▼71

74. One of the outcomes of the 'No-Go' areas in Belfast was that local 'vigilantes' took over the administration of law-and-order and via 'kangeroo courts' imposed punishment like this – tarring and feathering. (*Daily Mirror*)
75. But rapport continued. (*Daily Mirror*)

▲76 ▼77

76. An 'opening gambit' in Derry on 'Bloody Sunday', 30 January 1972. Troops face demonstrators before the shooting broke out. (*Daily Mirror*)

77. A picture that perhaps sums up the total futility of the 'Bloody Sunday' affair more than many others published in the past. A man lies dead, another lies wounded. An ambulance-man holds up a white flag. (Stan Matchett, *Daily Mirror*)

78. On 15 February 1972 *The Times* published this picture feature on its front page. The intention was to remind, or perhaps shock, the nation into an appreciation of the seriousness of the problem. The compiler of this book was involved in the project and insisted that no pictures be published without the full permission of the nearest relatives of the dead soldiers. Only one next-of-kin withheld permission. The picture of the 50th soldier to be killed, Private T. McCann, aged 19, of the Royal Army Ordnance Corps, could not be obtained in time. (Courtesy *The Times*)

▲79 ▼80

▼81

79. Results of an IRA bomb explosion at Great Victoria Street Station in the heart of Belfast on 22 March 1972. (Fred Hoare, *Daily Mirror*)

80. On 24 March 1972 the British Government announced Direct Rule in Northern Ireland after Mr Brian Faulkner's Government had said it would not accept loss of law-and-order powers. This prompted a demonstration by about 100,000 Protestants outside the Stormont Parliament buildings. On the same day (28 March) two people were killed by a bomb in Limavady and two Protestants were wounded by IRA snipers in Belfast. (*Daily Mirror*)

81. In April 1972, a Roman Catholic, Mr Joseph McCann, was shot dead in a fire fight involving British troops. Five civilians, including an eight-year-old boy, and a soldier were wounded in the same incident. Mr McCann's body lay in state for some time in the Turf Lodge district of Belfast. Widespread disturbances followed including this burning lorry barricade incident. (Cyril Cain, *Daily Mirror*)

▲82   ▼83

82. A 'No-Go' area. A Derry resident goes about his normal business with local law-and-order imposed by others shown on the right of the picture. (Henshaw Collection)

83. In 1971 and 1972 'private armies' on the Protestant side formed themselves up to counter threats from the IRA. An Ulster Defence Association 'patrol' in the Willowifield district of Belfast in May 1972. (Stanley Matchett, *Daily Mirror*)

84. In June 1972 a 'truce' was declared by both wings of the IRA. Lance-Corporal Paul Coombes of 3rd Battalion, The Royal Anglian Regiment celebrates it on a swing with Catholic children in the Falls Road area. He said to reporters at the time: 'It's like a different world now.' (Cyril Cain, *Daily Mirror*)

85. Meanwhile, a scene on Lough Erne. (Northern Ireland Tourist Board)

85

▼84

49

86. Typical bomb damage with soldiers on guard, Belfast 1972. (Henshaw Collection)
87. But children still have fun. A sack race in a Republican area of Belfast in the summer of 1972. (Peter Price, *Daily Mirror*)
88. A 'troops-and-crowd confrontation' in Belfast in July 1972. Note the British troop's equipment at this stage — rifles slung, helmets with visors, flak jackets, shields and batons. (Fred Hoare, *Dairy Mirror*)
89. Reminiscent of street fighting scenes during the Second World War. Troops in the gardens of houses in the Catholic Lenadoon Estate, July 1972. (George Phillips, *Daily Mirror*)

86

▼87

90. Children come first. Somewhere in Ulster, July 1972. (*Daily Mirror*)
91. But children remain involved. (Cyril Cain, *Daily Mirror*)
92. A children's 'game', July 1972. (*Daily Mirror*)
93. UDA post in Belfast, July 1972. (Cyril Cain, *Daily Mirror*)

90

▼**91**

▲92 ▼93

▲ 94

▼ 96

97. An anti-riot weapon first called 'the baton round', then the 'rubber bullet' and finally the 'plastic bullet', has been the subject of much controversy. British troops are seen here firing rubber bullets in Armagh in 1972. It is claimed that if used properly the rubber or plastic bullet has the advantage of keeping rioters and security forces apart, thus avoiding loss of temper and control; that unlike CS gas it is 'discriminatory' whereas the latter is more likely to affect the innocent, especially the very old and the very young. Again, if used properly it should NOT be lethal, probably inflicting no more serious injury than might be sustained in a rough game of Rugby football. Used *improperly*, however, it can: (a) blind if aimed too high, and (b) kill if used at too close a range. Numerous instances of both forms of misuse have been alleged against both the British Army and the RUC. The subject became an emotive one on the mainland during 1985 and 1986 because of the desire by a number of Chief Constables to have these weapons in their possession, and opposition to them expressed by a number of Police Committees. In studying this picture it is important to remember that the discharger 'kicks up', as does a pistol, a split second after firing. The soldier on the right of the group has probably fired first and his weapon *appears* to be aimed high, but was probably on the same line-of-sight as that of the man on the extreme left, who has not yet fired. (Henshaw Collection; RUC)

94. UDA press conference, July 1972. (Chris Paterson, *Daily Mirror*)

95. The bombers move out into the country. Damage in the little market town of Claudy in August 1972. Eight people were killed. (*Daily Mirror*)

96. At the end of July 1972 the British Army entered 'No-Go' areas of Belfast and Derry in what was styled Operation 'Motorman'. A scene in the Catholic Anderstown district of Belfast. (Fred Hoare, *Daily Mirror*)

▲95   ▼97

98. A bomb 'caught in the act' by the camera. This was a relatively minor incident during November 1972 in College Square, Belfast. The bomb had been placed in the car-park below the offices of an insurance company and of the Northern Ireland Housing Executive. A warning had been given, troops were standing by (see Army vehicle in bottom left-hand corner) and no one was in fact injured. A lot of paperwork had to be re-written, however. (Fred Hoare, *Daily Mirror*)

99. Whatever else happens, policemen still give comfort to distressed citizens. The aftermath of a bomb explosion in Belfast city centre in 1972. (Henshaw Collection)

100. During the annual Festival of Remembrance for the dead of two world wars in Belfast in November 1972, others remembered their dead in the current conflict. A mother and daughter plant a cross in remembrance of a son and brother. (Cyril Cain, *Daily Mirror*)

101. Into 1973. A fairly standard scene in Durham Street, Belfast of a combined Army/RUC check-point. Although 'soft hats' are being worn the policemen are wearing flak jackets. (Henshaw Collection)

102. The result of a bomb in 1973. The main shopping complex at Armagh. (Henshaw Collection)

▲101 ▼102

103. A combined operation, *circa* 1972/73. A policeman and a soldier arrest a terrorist gunman. His weapon lies on the pavement and the Lance-Corporal is in the act of getting it out of harm's way. This was an actual incident and not a 'still' from a TV thriller. (Henshaw Collection)

104. But. In June 1973 what was termed as 'The Coleraine Massacre' took place. Six people were killed in the first attack on this country town and 33 were injured. (*Daily Mirror*)

105. Meanwhile. The Strangford Lough ferry plied to and fro. (Northern Ireland Tourist Board)

▲103   ▼104

105

106. A march by members of the UDA in 1973. (*Daily Mirror*)

The consolidation of violence, 1973–8

The five-year period 1973–8 could be labelled as that of the 'Consolidation of Violence'. It was a period in which many political solutions were sought and explored, almost all really coming to naught, but one in which some of the most horrific acts of violence occurred. It was a period in which hundreds of totally innocent people lost their lives, their health, and occasionally their sanity.

It was, perhaps, a period in which the Irish Republican movement displayed itself at its worst, when in a hasty over-expansion of its 'military wing', i.e., the Provisional IRA, it had recruited too many people who actually *enjoyed* killing, wounding and torturing. This can happen to any nation, to any army, unless very great care is taken.

It was a period in which the Security Forces, led by the British Regular Army, grew wiser, more skilful and better equipped. It was also a period in which the 'indigenous' Security Forces, the RUC and the UDR, took an increasing share of the burden.

In order to explain this period it is perhaps best to list the events under the headings of (a) violence; (b) political manoeuvres; and (c) security measures.

Events of Violence between 1973 and 1978 can be catalogued as follows.

1973
January: Two car bombs exploded in London, killing one man and injuring 180 people.

1974
May: Twenty-two people killed in Dublin by car bombs which exploded without warning. Five killed by car bomb in Monaghan town.

November: Nineteen killed (mostly young people) and 182 injured when bombs were detonated in two Birmingham clubs; perhaps the worst, but almost forgotten, outrage committed by Republican extremists, either in Ulster or on the mainland. The long trial at Lancaster Castle proved that all the victims were totally innocent young people and that the perpetrators were a gang of incompetent, half-drunk, IRA 'agents' who had been supplied with weaponry and who had disobeyed so-called 'orders' to attack 'hard targets' and instead got rid of their bombs on a very 'soft target' before attempting to escape. They were caught – by astute police officers of the Lancashire Constabulary – when they tried to board a ferry at Heysham.

1975

April: Seven killed and 75 injured in two pub bombings in Belfast.

July: Three members of the 'Miami Showband' killed and one injured in an attack attributed to the UVF (Ulster Volunteer Force). Two UVF members also died, blowing themselves up, in the same attack.

October: Twelve people, including three women and four UVF men, killed and 46 injured, in a series of UVF attacks.

1976

January: Five Roman Catholics killed in two separate incidents near Whitecross, South Armagh. Ten Protestant workers shot dead at Kingsmills, South Armagh. (An organization calling itself the 'Republic Action Force' claimed responsibility for this outrage.)

May: Three RUC men killed by a bomb at Belcoo, Co. Fermanagh.

August: Mr Gerry Fitt, MP, had to fight off Republican demonstrators trying to enter his own home. He used his pistol to good effect.

1976

October: Mrs Maire Drumm, vice-president of the Provisional Sinn Fein (political wing of the Provisional IRA) was shot dead in the Mater Hospital, Belfast, where she was a patient.

1977

July: Four killed and eighteen injured in Belfast in a feud between Provisional and Official IRA elements.

December: Five Ulster hotels damaged by IRA fire-bombs.

1978

February: Twelve killed and 23 injured when the La Mont restaurant in Co. Down was destroyed by Provisional IRA fire-bombs.

The main political events which occurred during this period included:

1973

March: The British Government published a White Paper proposing an Assembly, to be elected by Proportional Representation, but with Westminster retaining law-and-order powers. Polling took place for the above in June 1973.

November: Agreement was reached in Stormont talks on the setting-up of a power-sharing Executive.

December: A conference at Sunningdale was attended by British and Irish ministers and by representatives of the Northern Ireland 'power-sharing' parties.

1974

January: The 'Northern Ireland Executive' took office. Three days later the Ulster Unionist Council rejected the 'Council of Ireland' proposed at the Sunningdale talks, and

three days after that Mr Brian Faulkner resigned as Unionist Party leader. He did, however, visit Dublin for talks with the Taoiseach, Mr Liam Cosgrave, on 16 January.

1974

March: The Labour Party took office in the UK and Mr Merlyn Rees became Secretary of State for Northern Ireland.

May: The power-sharing Executive won an Assembly vote on the Sunningdale Agreement, but almost immediately the Loyalist Ulster Workers' Council brought about power cuts and strikes. The Unionist members of the Executive resigned and this organization collapsed. Direct Rule was resumed.

1975

Numerous political manoeuvres took place including the creation of a 'Convention' and a personal visit by Harold Wilson, then Prime Minister, to Derry. All these events were, however, outstripped by the acts of violence listed above.

1976

March: A final sitting of the 'Convention' ended in uproar and it was formally dissolved by a Westminster Order.

August: Brian Faulkner resigned from active politics.

September: The European Commission on Human Rights decided that Britain had been guilty of torturing internees in 1971, but said that internment had been justified.

1976

September: Mr Roy Mason succeeded Mr Merlyn Rees as Secretary of State for Northern Ireland.

1977

March: Brian Faulkner, by then Lord Faulkner of Downpatrick, was killed when he fell from his horse while hunting.

May: A body called the 'United Unionist Action Council' (UUAC) promoted another 'Loyalist Strike' involving power-stations and some factories. This was to become a familiar feature of 'Loyalist' reaction to political developments, and was repeated up to March 1986.

1978

January: The European Court of Human Rights in Strasbourg proclaimed that interrogation techniques used on internees in 1971 did not amount to torture, but had been 'inhuman and degrading'.

During this five-year period the roles of the Security Forces changed dramatically. For the British Regular Army it was a period in which priorities changed from techniques for controlling street riots to street-*fighting* techniques, and indeed to rural *fighting* techniques. The Army moved on from a period in which it had tried to be a type

of police force into one in which it was taking on guerrilla warfare, for which perhaps, it was better equipped, by both training and tradition.

Not only did the 'enemy' gunmen, in the form of increasingly better-armed Provisional IRA members have to be taken on and defeated, but just as importantly the bombers had to be taken on and defeated. The special role played by the bomb-disposal experts will be described in more detail later, but the war against the bombers meant that Intelligence gathering had to take very high priority in British Army operations.

During this five-year period too, all branches of the Security Forces learned to work together, and enjoyed working together. The Regular British Army 'force level' had reached a peak of 22,000 in 1972, but it became possible to taper this off, stage by stage, as the form of the conflict changed, and as the RUC and the Ulster Defence Force became able to take on greater responsibilities.

The casualty figures for the period 1973–8 were appalling – a total of 1,204 dead, including 756 civilians, presumably all of these innocent and uncommitted civilians. These figures brought the 'grand' – if such a word should properly be used – of deaths in the current conflict to 1,871. At the end of this period the statistical deadline of '2,000 Deaths' was not far away.

107. The morning after a rough night in the Falls Road/Leeson Street area in 1973. (Henshaw Collection)
108. The results of a land-mine on the Border, 1973. (Henshaw Collection)

109. The old and the young in the Border town of Newtownhamilton, 1973. (Henshaw Collection)
110. Harland & Wolff went on building ships. (Harland & Wolff)

▲109   ▼110

11. Crumlin Road prison, Belfast, with special protection, 1973. (Henshaw Collection)

12. The Grand Central Hotel Royal Avenue, Belfast. Once a place of delight for bon viveurs, including journalists with expense accounts; by 1973 a fortified barrack block for troops on duty in the city centre. Later demolished to make room for a £40m shopping complex. (Henshaw Collection)

▲111   ▼112

◀113   ▲114   ▼115

▼116

113. Terrorism with little apparent reason. On 1 February 1974 two Electricity Board workmen were shot dead in their tin hut shelter on the outskirts of Belfast; another three were wounded. There were thirteen men in the hut. Two masked men demanded to see their pay-packets then ordered the Protestants to kneel down in front and the rest to stand at the back. A machine-gun and a pistol were used. The two dead were both Catholics. (Cyril Cain, *Daily Mirror*)

114. Belfast graffiti, 1974. (Cyril Cain, *Daily Mirror*)

115. In October 1973 a freight train was hijacked on a level crossing by masked gunmen two miles from the Border near Armagh. The driver and crew were ordered out, and mail and newspapers destroyed by a bomb. Photographers and reporters narrowly escaped injury in a second bomb probably intended for Army bomb-disposal teams. (Stanley Matchett, *Daily Mirror*)

116. Another sad scene on Remembrance Day in Belfast, November 1973. Andrea Schrader, then aged 5, plants a cross in memory of her dead uncle. (Stanley Matchett, *Daily Mirror*)

▲117 ▼118

117. An Army bulldozer lifts a burning bus from a road-block in the Falls Road during 'disturbances' in August 1974. (Henshaw Collection)

118. Bombings and other forms of nastiness were not confined to the 'working-class areas'. A bomb alert in progress in an 'upper middle-class' area of Belfast in 1974. (Henshaw Collection)

119. UVF press conference, October 1974. (Cyril Cain, *Daily Mirror*)

120. Priests administer the last rites to a bomb victim in 1974. (Henshaw Collection via RUC)

▲119   ▼120

121. In the midst of the conflict, it is often forgotten that it is still the Royal National Lifeboat Institution which provides and mans, on a voluntary basis, all the lifeboats on the coasts of Ireland, both North and South. This picture shows the Newcastle (Co. Down) lifeboat *William and Laura* in action. (Courtesy RNLI. Picture by Bill Hamilton) During the period 1970–85, the 26 deep-sea and inshore lifeboats were launched on 2,862 occasions, usually in appalling weather, and saved a total of 1,177 lives. 'The Border' has never divided the work of the Royal National Lifeboat Institution. RN and RAF rescue helicopters often overfly Irish airspace and refuel on Irish territory during life-saving missions. Close, if informal, relations exist between the British Armed Forces and the Irish Army Air Corps rescue helicopter crew and many lives have been saved under this arrangement. (Courtesy RNLI)

▲121 ▼122

22. For the British Army it has now become 'a real war'. A 'rural patrol' leaving Newtownhamilton in early 1975. (Henshaw Collection)

23. A gun battle broke out in the Divis Street area in August 1975. A six-year-old girl was killed in crossfire and the inevitable confrontations with Security Forces ensued. (Cyril Cain, *Daily Mirror*)

24. Cross-Border co-operation. A British officer makes contact with the Gardai somewhere along the Border. (Henshaw Collection)

▲123 ▼124

125. Another scene from the Divis Street gunfight in August 1975. (Cyril Cain, *Daily Mirror*)

126. Meanwhile – summer in Northern Ireland. (Northern Ireland Tourist Board)

127. Some deliberate attempt were made to disrupt the still successful tourist trade. In August 1976 eight bombs were exploded in Portrush, Ulster's 'mini Blackpool'. Ice-cream parlours, shops and an amusement arcade were destroyed, happily without loss of life. (Fred Hoare, *Daily Mirror*)

128. And young people still enjoyed themselves, even in the middle of Belfast. Canoeing on the River Lagan. (Northern Ireland Tourist Board)

125

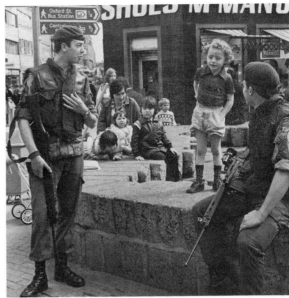

◄129　▲130　　　　　　　　　　　　　▲131

132　　　　　　　　　　　　　　　　　133

129. A sign of hope in November 1976. Young 'Peace People' taking part in a candlelit march through Belfast.

130. 'The Peace Women', Mairead Corrigan and Betty Williams, with Paul Joans in centre. (Stanley Matchett, *Daily Mirror*)

131. Even in 1977 soldiers and children could be friends in the centre of Belfast. Note, however, that despite the relaxed atmosphere the soldier on the left still has his rifle strapped to his wrist. (Henshaw Collection)

132. 'A soldier's job is never done'. A demonstration of military versatility in Belfast city centre in 1977. (Henshaw Collection)

133. At the same time children had uglier things to observe. The aftermath of a car bomb in the Ardoyne district of Belfast in 1977. (Henshaw Collection)

▲134

▲135 ▼136

▲137 ▼138

134. A joint Army/RUC patrol in the Ardoyne district of Belfast in 1977. (Henshaw Collection)

135. Belfast city centre *circa* 1977 with security/search gates and armed troops at the ready. (Henshaw Collection)

136. A sort of a Christmas greeting from the IRA on 21 December 1977. A shop in Royal Avenue, Belfast, stocked with gifts and greetings cards explodes after two gunmen had walked in, given a warning, and deposited a bomb, saying: 'That's a little present from your friendly Provos'. There were no casualties. (Fred Hoare, *Daily Mirror*)

137. A helicopter's view of the centre of Belfast, *circa* 1978. (The aircraft is a Gazelle of No. 653 Squadron, Army Air Corps). (Henshaw Collection)

138. By the turn of 1978 the IRA were 'into' such weapons as mortars and rocket launchers. The remains of a mortar launching vehicle used at Forkhill to wound three policemen and eight soldiers. (Fred Hoare, *Daily Mirror*)

139. The Belfast Fire Brigade in action, 1978. (Henshaw Collection)
140. Soldiers and firemen tackle the results of a fire-bomb in Belfast in 1978. The part played by *firemen* throughout the Northern Ireland conflict has gone almost unrecorded and has perhaps been underrated. They have always remained 'neutral', have often displayed great gallantry, and many have been attacked and injured while trying to carry out humanitarian tasks. (Henshaw Collection)
141. Typical bomb damage in the centre of Omagh in November 1978. (Henshaw Collection)
142. Milk churn bombs 'in transit'; discovered under soil in the back of a lorry, 1978. (Henshaw Collection)

◄139 ▲140

▲141 ▼142

143. 'Waiting for the bang'. Troops and policemen protect their ears while a bomb is about to be subjected to a 'controlled explosion' in the centre of Belfast in 1978. (Henshaw Collection)

144. Meanwhile, industry went on, especially high technology precision engineering. A shot taken in the Cameo works at Monkstown.

'An acceptable level of violence', 1978–

he period from 1978 up to the time of writing (1986) may be regarded in retrospect as one in which an 'acceptable level of violence' (as predicted, to much derision, by Mr Reginald Maudling in 1970) was at least achieved. In viewing this description of the period it does, of course, depend on what one means by 'acceptable'.

The atrocities and outrages continued, spreading even more frequently to the mainland, but year by year the casualties among uninvolved and uncommitted civilians declined; the 'war' becoming a more clearly defined one between the terrorists and the Security Forces, with soldiers and policemen the main targets. Politicians and their families remained 'hard targets' however.

There was a general reduction in crude street rioting with its accompanying damage to the property of innocent people, but the weapons available to the terrorists and used by them became more and more sophisticated. The latter, however, were met by increasing skills and counter-weapons in the hands of the Security Forces.

The British Regular Army was able to reduce its 'Force Levels'; making more use of its semi-permanently based units on two-and-a-half-year terms accompanied by families, and making less demands on other units for four-month 'emergency' or 'roulement' tours which had imposed special strains during the period 1969–75.

During this period, however, a new force, INLA (Irish National Liberation Army) made its presence felt. Initially the military wing of the IRSP (Irish Republican Socialist Party), itself a breakaway from the 'Official' Sinn Fein, it emerged from 1975 onwards as a particularly ruthless paramilitary group with strained relations – if there were any relations at all – with the Provisional IRA.

From 1979 onwards the responsibility for atrocities had to be distinguished between those committed by the Provos (PIRA) and those by the INLA. Sometimes, but not always, one or other would 'claim responsibility', usually in the form of an anonymous telephone message to the Press Association.

It was also a period in which the hunger-strikers and other protesters (including the 'dirty strikers') within the Maze Prison were successful in propaganda moves which led to many Irish Americans, perhaps not fully understanding the situation from 5,000 or more miles away, sending financial and other support to what they saw as a legitimate cause.

There follows a list (by no means a complete one) of the atrocities committed between 1979 and the time of writing:

1979
March: On 30 March the Conservative spokesman on Northern Ireland Affairs, Mr Airey Neave, MP, was killed when a bomb exploded under his car in the Westminster House of Commons car-park. The INLA claimed responsibility.

April: Four policemen were killed at Bessbrook, Co, Armagh, when a 1,000lb bomb exploded in a van as they were passing in a Land Rover.

August: Eighteen British Regular Army soldiers were killed on 27 August at Warrenpoint by PIRA bombers. This was the highest death-toll in a single incident of violence. In the same month Earl Mountbatten of Burma was murdered, together with his 14-year-old grandson and a boy crewman by a radio-triggered explosion in his boat at Mullaghmore, Co. Sligo.

December: Five British soldiers were killed by a PIRA land-mine.

1980
January: Three people were killed in a terrorist train explosion at Dunmurry.

August: Three people were killed and eighteen injured in widespread violence on the ninth anniversary of internment.

1981
May: Bobby Sands, MP, died on the 66th day of his fast in prison. There was rioting in Belfast, Derry and Dublin and 600 extra troops were sent to Northern Ireland. After ensuing violence five British soldiers were killed when their Saracen was blown up by a land-mine near Bessbrook.

August: Hunger-striker Kieran Doherty, TD, died. During subsequent violence two people died in Belfast and it was estimated that more than 1,000 petrol bombs were thrown at Security Forces.

September: Two policemen were killed by a PIRA land-mine near Pomeroy.

October: One woman killed and 23 soldiers plus seventeen civilians injured by remotely controlled nail bomb outside the Chelsea Barracks in London.

1982
March: An 11-year-old boy killed and 34 people injured,

some seriously, by a bomb which exploded without warning in Banbridge.

April: Two killed, twelve injured and £1m damage caused by PIRA bomb attacks in Belfast, Derry, Armagh, Strabane, Ballymena, Bessbrook and Magharafelt.

June: In New York the FBI arrested four men said to have tried to buy 'Redeye' surface-to-air missiles for the Provisional IRA.

July: Eight soldiers killed and 51 people injured by two Provisional IRA bombs in London. One bomb exploded near the Household Cavalry Barracks at Knightsbridge, the other at the Regent's Park bandstand. Three others died later.

October: Three policemen killed by a booby-trapped land-mine near Lurgan.

December: Seventeen people, including eleven soldiers, died in INLA bombing of the 'Droppin' Well' public house and disco club outside the former RAF, latterly Army, base at Ballykelly, Co. Londonderry.

1983

January: Two policemen shot dead by PIRA in Rostrevor, Co. Down.

July: Four UDR men killed by a PIRA land-mine in Co. Tyrone – this Regiment's heaviest loss in a single incident.

And so the atrocities went on, both in Ireland and in the rest of the British Isles, perhaps culminating in the attack aimed at the Prime Minister, Mrs Thatcher, but in fact killing and injuring 'softer' political targets at Brighton in 1984.

Political moves by both the British and Irish governments went on apace during this period. Most of them came to naught because of the continuing undercurrent of violence. Below are listed some of the highlights of the attempts to achieve a 'political solution'.

1979

May: A Conservative Government under the Premiership of Mrs Margaret Thatcher was returned to power, with Mr Humphrey Atkin succeeding Mr Roy Mason as Northern Ireland Secretary.

1980

January: A Constitutional Conference was opened at Stormont.

March: The Constitutional Conference was adjourned indefinitely with no sign of agreement.

May: The SDLP leader, Mr John Hume, met Mrs Thatcher at 10 Downing Street. Mrs Thatcher and Mr Haughey, then Prime Minister of the Irish Republic, met at 10 Downing Street.

1980

June: The European Commission of Human Rights rejected the case of protesting H-Block (Maze Prison) prisoners, finding that the debasement arising from the

'dirty protest' was self-inflicted. Nevertheless the Commission criticized the British Government for inflexibility.

1981

November: Mrs Thatcher and the newly elected Irish Premier, Dr Garret Fitzgerald, decided to hold London talks with a view to setting up an 'Inter-Governmental Council'.

1982

March: On a St Patrick's Day visit to the United States, the re-elected Taoiseach of the Irish Republic said that the United States Government should bring more pressure on Britain to adopt a more positive attitude to Irish Unity. President Reagan said that any solution must come from the Northern Ireland people themselves.

November: The Queen's Speech at the opening of Parliament re-affirmed the Government's intention to carry on with 'the Assembly'.

And so have continued the political manoeuvrings to the time of writing. The Anglo-Irish Agreement was put forward in 1985 with predictable reactions from the 'Loyalists' culminating in a planned one-day strike which in March 1986 turned into a one-day episode of violence reminiscent of the early riots of the late 1960s.

At the time of writing it was easy for any 'Ulster-Watcher' to become totally cynical. This compiler had become hopeful when on a '10-years-After' assignment he had been able, in 1978, to record how the places where he had seen horrible violence, had again become normal parts of a normal community. Yet every now and again the clock and the calendar seemed to be turned back. Again and again the news items included details of policemen or soldiers being killed. These incidents seldom made the 'main news' item on the BBC radio news, yet depressingly often they were repeated in the 'headlines'.

Perhaps by 1986 the 'Acceptable Level of Violence' had been achieved. Some of the statistics below may tell their own story if interpreted correctly. Nevertheless it should never be forgotten, as said in the outset of this book, that a great many people in Northern Ireland have lived, and continue to live, normally, happy, healthy lives. Perhaps very importantly they are always ready to welcome the rest of us as their friends and guests. Long may that arrangement continue.

Again in this last period under review the casualty statistics remain frightening, with 672 deaths in all groups recorded between 1979 and 1985, bringing the 'grand total' to 2,462. This means that give or take additional deaths from the time of writing, at least 2,500 lives will have been lost in the 'conflict' by the time this book appears.

A breakdown of the death statistics between 1979 and 1986 is, however, significant, and indeed perhaps encouraging. Deaths of British Regular soldiers fell from 38 in 1979 to only two in 1985. Deaths among policemen rose, however, to 23 in 1985 compared with nine in 1980.

Deaths among UDR soldiers reached thirteen in 1981 but dropped to five in 1985. Civilian deaths remained at a distressingly high level, and this of course is the field in which one could put, or not put, an assessment of whether an acceptable level of violence' had been reached. Forty-eight civilians were killed in 1979; 45 in 1970; this sad figure dropping to what perhaps could be called a 'low' of twenty in 1985.

By 1986, therefore, there was nothing for anyone to be complacement about in terms of statistics, although perhaps there were other signs of hope.

In February 1986 Richard Ford, *The Times* staff correspondent in Northern Ireland, was able to write a 'Letter from Belfast' recording the delights of eating out, of club- and theatre-going in Belfast, and describing how the wire-mesh search-and-security fences in the city centre had been demolished. He was able to record that £86m had been invested in a new shopping centre and many more millions were on their way for other ideas.

Writing or commenting on a 'moving situation' is always a dangerous practice, especially when the time lapse between the last word written and the appearance of that word before a reader, is a necessarily long one in terms of the production of a book, rather than that of a daily newspaper.

This compiler can only conclude his comments on the time-phased sections of this book by saying that *he* lives in hope for a community in which he lived for many months and which he came to love.

145. That standard item of farming equipment, the milk-churn, was often turned into a highly lethal bomb. Officers of The Royal Greenjackets make a check with a farmer near the Border in 1979. (Henshaw Collection)

146. It is very difficult to keep children away. A scene in the Falls Road area of Belfast in 1979. (Henshaw Collection)
147. So what is it all about? (Henshaw Collection)

▲146 ▼147

148. Whatever else may happen, Northern Ireland is not immune from natural disasters; serious flooding occurred in October 1980. The soldiers, as usual, did their best to help. (Cyril Cain, *Daily Mirror*)

149. And the soldiers and the children continued to be friends, in May 1981. (David Caulkin, *Daily Mirror*)

149

150. But a constant guard had to be maintained. Lance-Corporal Poyner of 1st Royal Greenjackets in a 'covert' Observation Post near Crossmaglen. (Henshaw Collection)

151. A scene from the constant 'Battle on the Border', *circa* 1981. A specialist team of Royal Engineers with a specialist dog. (Henshaw Collection)

152. Soldiers and members of the Women's Royal Army Corps on routine duty in Belfast, *circa* 1983. (Henshaw Collection)

153. Family life in Belfast in 1984. Women walk home, a child looks out of the window and a soldier of the 3rd Royal Greenjackets remains on cautious guard. (Henshaw Collection)

▲150

152

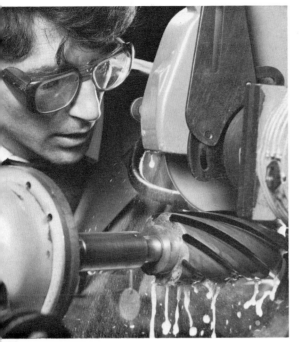

156

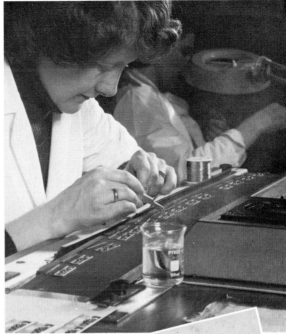

157

154. Industry went on. The name of 'Shorts' will always be revered in the aviation world, with that of the 'Short Sunderland' flying-boat absolutely immortal. A recent product, the Short 360 36-seat 'regional airliner'. Since entering commercial operation in December 1982, it has been adopted by 22 carriers worldwide with orders and options placed for many more.

155. The *Auckland Star*, built and launched at Harland & Wolff, on sea trials in Belfast Lough.

156. A scene in the works of Maydown Precision Engineering Ltd, Derry.

157. More precision work – at Stability Electronics, Antrim.

158. But nothing much had changed in the Lower Falls by 1984. (Henshaw Collection)

158

▲159　▼160

▼161

▲162   ▼163

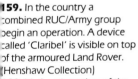

159. In the country a combined RUC/Army group begin an operation. A device called 'Claribel' is visible on top of the armoured Land Rover. (Henshaw Collection)

160. Various branches of the Armed/Security Forces were sometimes called in to assist in local problems. A cow in distress can be seen being put into a net with assistance of the local soldiery. (Henshaw Collection)

161. And then being lifted to safety by an RAF Wessex helicopter. (Henshaw Collection)

162. A fairly typical morning for a soldier of 3rd Greenjackets in West Belfast, 1984. (Henshaw Collection)

163. But one still cannot keep the children away. A meeting between soldiers of 3rd Royal Greenjackets and a resident of West Belfast in 1984. (Henshaw Collection)

164. A border scene in 1985. This was an INLA (Irish National Liberation Army) assassination. (Henshaw Collection)

165. How to derail a train. Charges placed against the main Dublin–Belfast line in 1985. The hand of a Royal Army Ordnance Corps ATO (Ammunition Technical Officer) can be seen at bottom left. (Henshaw Collection)

166. Towards the turn of the decade 1970–1980, the UDR were playing an increasingly important part in Security operations, thereby releasing Regular British Army units from commitments they were finding it hard to meet. An 'Urban Patrol' of the UDR. (Henshaw Collection)

167. From the beginning, women joined, and played a major part in all the operations of the UDR. They cheerfully adopted the nickname of 'Greenfinches'. What can best be described as a closely linked patrol. Note in top right-hand corner another example of close-linking – a soldier and his dog. (Henshaw Collection)

▲165   ▼166

▼167

168. As for all 'reserve forces', a problem for the UDR was keeping fit. Volunteers on a 'walk-and-run' exercise. (Henshaw Collection)

169. Inside a UDR Observation Post. (Henshaw Collection)

170. At an early stage, the Regiment was equipped with the Ulster-built Shorland light armoured cars, earlier used by the RUC. (Henshaw Collection)

▲168 ▼169

▼170

171. Soldiers of the UDR were quickly trained in modern methods of troop deployment. 'Emplaning' into a Royal Air Force helicopter. (Henshaw Collection)

172. And 'deplaning' from a Royal Air Force Wessex Support helicopter. (Henshaw Collection)

▲171 ▼172

173. But many UDR volunteers, especially the 'part-timers', have died and, at the date of writing these words, continue to die at the hands of their opponents. Mr Stephen Carlton, a worker at a filling-station in Antrim Road, Belfast, and a part-time member of the UDR, lies dead on 8 January 1982, in the forecourt of his garage. He was shot eight times in the body, head and legs by two gunmen. (Henshaw Collection)

174. The remains of a UDR volunteer and a Mini in Belfast in August 1982. An example of what was to become a familiar scene. (Henshaw Collection)

173 ▼174

175. Meanwhile – a good, safe paddling beach at Downhill, Co. Londonderry. (Northern Ireland Tourist Board)

▲176 ▼177

176. Aftermath of the Warrenpoint attack on British troops in which eighteen soldiers died on 27 August 1979. (Henshaw Collection)
177. An aerial view of the Warrenpoint calamity. (Henshaw Collection)
178. The Marina Hotel at Ballycastle, bombed in June 1979. (Henshaw Collection)
179. Meanwhile, summer holidays went on at Portrush. (Northern Ireland Tourist Board)

178   ▼179

180. But a bomb exploded in the middle of Ballymena. (Henshaw Collection)
181. A 300-pound car bomb in Omagh. (Henshaw Collection)
182. A bomb in Castlederg. (Henshaw Collection)
183. A bomb in Dungannon. (Henshaw Collection)

▲181 ▼182

▼183

184. But Belfast's Grand Opera House was re-opened in 1980. (Central Office of Information)

185. New housing was built (Central Office of Information)

186. And the Belfast City Marathon was resumed in the 1980s. (Northern Ireland Tourist Board)

◄184 ▲185 ▼186

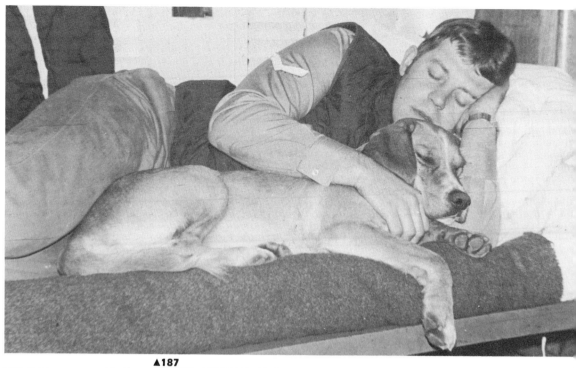

▲187

187. But temporary residents had to sleep where they could. (Henshaw Collection)

188, 189. Other temporary residents had to get on with their jobs. (Henshaw Collection)

190. And normal life resumed in Belfast. (Northern Ireland Tourist Board)

189

▲188 ▼190

Security forces weapons and equipment

For the most part the equipment and weapons used by the Security Forces, particularly those used by the British Regular Army, were designed for battle against an equally well-armed enemy rather than specifically for internal security duties.

The following pictures illustrate a selection of vehicles, some armoured, some 'semi-armoured', others in the military 'soft vehicle' category, used by all branches of the Security Forces. As stated in some of the picture captions and earlier narratives, the use of any form of tracked vehicle, even a bulldozer, which could be classified as a 'tank' has almost always been studiously avoided.

The British Army's basic personal weapon, the 7.62mm self-loading rifle has always been a difficult one to use in close-quarter street-fighting and internal security duties, partly because its velocity is such that it can kill up to three people standing behind one another at medium range or penetrate a house wall behind which an innocent person might be standing. It is also impossible to use it under any 'shoot to wound' orders because the high-velocity impact of its bullet even on a leg or shoulder can set up lethal shock waves through the nervous system. ('Shooting to wound' and 'firing over the heads' have never in fact been practical methods of riot control as they usually result in innocent people being killed, thereby making the political situation even worse.)

Numerous other weapons and devices have, of course, been invented during the Northern Ireland conflict, some still classified, others illustrated in the following pages. Much improvisation has taken place, as it always has done in events involving the British armed forces.

Perhaps the most significant advances in martial arts in Northern Ireland have taken place in the field of 'bomb disposal'. When the Ulster conflict moved into the high-explosives era in 1970, the general public still associated the art of bomb disposal with the Corps of Royal Engineers, whose special units had dealt so efficiently and gallantly with unexploded bombs dropped by the Luftwaffe on Britain during the Second World War. It was not fully appreciated by the public that the responsibility for bomb, or high-explosives disposal and safety has always been divided into several parts within the armed forces. The Royal Engineers have been, and still are, responsible for explosive devices dropped by enemy aircraft and for land-mines. The Royal Navy has been, and still is, responsible for explosive devices at sea (i.e., mines) and for almost anything lying around on beaches up to high-water mark. The Royal Air Force is responsible fo explosives on its own airfields and of course on board it own aeroplanes.

Within the British Army, however, the often under-sun Royal Army Ordnance Corps is, and always has beer responsible for the safe-keeping and disposal of all othe types of explosive device, ranging from shells stored i ammunition depots to terrorist booby-traps.

When the IRA began to make and plant bombs fror 1970 onwards, steadily increasing the sophistication c their timing devices, it therefore became an RAOC responsibility to deal with them, and a rather special bree of soldiers, known as ATOs (Ammunition Technica Officers), some commissioned officers, others warran officers, moved into the limelight. The world owes much t them.

Part of their story has been well told by one of the greatest of them all, Lieutenant-Colonel George Styles GC, in his book *Bombs Have No Pity* (William Luscombe 1975). George Styles, whose award is equivalent to that o the VC, and his friends were the pioneers in the art o outwitting the IRA bomb-makers. Perhaps little more nee be said in a book of this sort than to quote the words o the citation for George Styles's decoration in 1972 and those of another citation which led to the award of the Wilkinson Sword of Peace to No. 321 Explosive Ordnanc Disposal Unit, Royal Army Ordnance Corps in 1978. The citation for George Styles's George Cross reads:

'As Senior Ammunition Technical Officer, Northern Ireland Major Styles was responsible for the supervision of the Explosive Ordnance Disposal teams in the Royal Army Ordnance Corps deployed to deal with the ever increasing number of explosive devices used in the terroris campaign.
On 20th October 1971 Major Styles was called to assis with a device of an apparently new design placed in a public telephone kiosk in Belfast's comparatively new, anc largest, hotel, The Europa.
Major Styles immediately went to the scene and, having ensured that the military and the police had secured the area and evacuation of personnel had also been effected took charge of the operation of neutralizing, removing and dismantling the bomb.
Investigation revealed that the bomb was of a new anc complicated construction with anti-handling devices tc defeat attempts to disarm it. Until the electrical circuit hac

91. A British soldier in 'riot gear' at the turn of 1969/70. He is still wearing a standard 'tin hat', and a respirator for protection against CS gas. The long baton enables him to engage rioters at close quarters and perhaps be a member of a 'snatch squad'. (Henshaw Collection)

been neutralized the slightest movement could have set it off.

The device contained between 10 and 15lb of explosive and could have caused instant death as well as extensive damage.

No one was more aware of the destructive capability of the bomb than Major Styles, yet he placed himself at great personal risk to minimize the danger to his team, to confirm the success of each stage of the operation and to ensure the practicability of the next stage. The whole operation took seven hours to plan and execute and was completely successful.

Two days later he was again called to the same hotel where a second bomb had been laid by armed terrorists. This bomb was found to be an even larger device with a charge of over 30lb of explosive, anti-handling devices, and a confusion of electrical circuits. It was clearly intended to defeat disarming techniques and to kill the operator trying to neutralize it.

Major Styles immediately took charge of the situation and successfully disarmed, removed and dismantled the bomb, this time after nine hours' intense and dangerous work.

As a result of his courageous and dedicated resolution, two determined and ingenious attempts by terrorists against life and property were defeated, and technical information was obtained which will help to save the lives of operators faced with the same devices in future.'

The Citation for the award of the Wilkinson Sword of Peace to 321 EOD Unit, RAOC read:

'Eight years ago, 321 EOD Unit RAOC was established in Northern Ireland to counter the terrorist bombing campaign. Its role is of a non-offensive protective nature, in that its actions are aimed solely at preventing loss of life and property.

It is self-evident that the operations of the Unit have saved human life, and there is no doubt that they have both prevented damage to a vast amount of property and helped to prevent terrorists achieving their aim of totally disrupting the economy and society of Northern Ireland.

Since 1969 and up until this year, the Unit has dealt with some 24,500 calls of which some 9,500 were to actual terrorist bombs. Of these actual bombs, 3,800 were successfully neutralized.

Up until April last year (1977) 398 ATOs (Ammunition Technical Officers) and ATs (Ammunition Technicians) have carried out EOD tours in Northern Ireland, including 45 second tours. Their successes have not been achieved without terrible cost, nor have they gone unrecognized. To date 16 EOD operators have been killed carrying out their duties and 10 injured, three seriously. Their gallantry has been recognized by the awards of one George Cross, three OBEs, six MBEs, 24 GMs (George Medals), 22 QMGs (Queen's Gallantry Medals), 15 BEMs (British Empire Medals), 31 Mentions in Dispatches and two General-Officer-Commanding Commendations.'

Some of those figures were up-dated at a presentation conducted early in 1986. They brought the total of George Medals up to 42, the OBEs to 11, the MBEs to 23, the QGNs to 41, the BEMs to 23 and the Mentions in Dispatches to 74. The deaths had also gone up to seventeen.

A new Mk 8 version of Wheelbarrow, radio-controlled and able to operate at greater ranges, was introduced into service early in 1986. It can work at a distance of 200 metres from its control van, compared with the 100-metre range of its cable-controlled predecessors. It can move at 5mph, twice as fast as its predecessors, has camera 'eyes' and an improved monitoring system.

The remaining pictures in this section show the weapons and explosive devices used by the IRA, the INLA and other organizations. The picture captions should be self-explanatory.

92. A fully equipped British Regular Army soldier in Ulster *circa* 1975, with standard NATO self-loading rifle and 'Night Sight'; flak-jacket; gas mask; and helmet with visor. A far cry from the 'tin hats' and batons of the turn of the decade. (Henshaw Collection)

93. During the late 1970s/early 1980s, the RUC took on an increasing share of security work and had to be appropriately equipped and trained. A policeman in full riot gear, carrying a 'plastic bullet' discharger and wearing body armour. (Henshaw Collection)

192

193

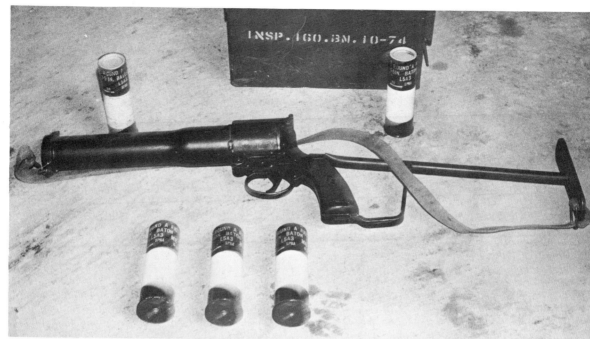

▲194 ▼195

▼196

194. The 'weapon' that has caused much distress and argument on both sides of the Irish Sea. A 1.5in 'discharger', capable of launching rubber or plastic 'bullets', and equally capable of launching CS gas canisters. First evolved during the First World War for the firing of Very Lights, it has been used for close on three-quarters of a century, often for the saving of life when used to fire distress flares; but in 1986 its use became the subject of much controversy when mainland Chief Constables considered it should be available to them in the event of their having to control violent riots. (Henshaw Collection)

195. A British soldier going into action with a 1.5in discharger, probably firing a 'rubber bullet', in training. Note that the discharger is aimed low and that the outcome should NOT be lethal. (Henshaw Collection)

196. The British soldier's personal equipment gradually built up from what it had been when he first arrived 'on the streets'. A soldier equipped with a visor attached to his standard 'tin hat', plus a riot shield, and a baton – the last perhaps fitting him to be a member of a 'snatch squad'. (Henshaw Collection)

197. Many improvements were made to the 'tin hat'. This is the 'Internal Security Combat Helmet'. (Henshaw Collection)

198. A typical British Army 'flak jacket', officially designated 'fragmentation vest'. (Henshaw Collection)

199. The British soldier's most important weapon during the gun-fighting phase of the Ulster problem. A standard NATO SLR (self-loading rifle) fitted with a telescopic sight. (Henshaw Collection)

197   **198**

199

200. From an early stage dogs played an important part in the whole security operation, their part in many a minor war having been proved over many years. Dogs are divided into 'Groundhogs', who, follow a scent, and 'Wagtails', who will sniff out explosives, and indeed drugs. This is a portrait of a 'Groundhog' following a scent. (Henshaw Collection)
201. Another 'Wagtail' in action, sniffing at a potential bomb. (Henshaw Collection)
202. A RUC dog with handler. (RUC)

200 ▲**201** ▼**202**

▲203 ▼204

203. In the late 1960s and early 1970s the British Army had to get to grips with the training of its soldiers for action in Ulster. A scene photographed at a training camp 'somewhere in the UK', with young soldiers playing the parts of potential demonstrators/rioters. (Henshaw Collection)

204. Another training scene enacted somewhere in the UK, complete with a 'Pig' (Humber Armoured Personnel Carrier), smoke, graffiti, and spent CS gas cartridges liberally sprinkled on the ground. (Henshaw Collection)

205. The RUC took an increasing part in security duties. A policeman provides armed cover to colleagues carrying out a vehicle check on the bridge in the background. (RUC)

206. Meanwhile, the RUC policemen went about 'ordinary coppers' business'. (RUC)

207. And there was no amnesty for speeding motorists. (RUC)

208. Meanwhile, the sewers of Belfast had to be watched. Sappers of the Corps of Royal Engineers 'about their business' somewhere underground. (Henshaw Collection)

▲205 ▼206

▼207   208 ►

▲209 ▼210

▼211

209. A Saracen armoured personnel carrier, widely used by the British Army throughout Ulster. As a battlefield infantry carrier the Saracen had been rated as obsolescent by 1969 and was about to be replaced by light tracked vehicles in the Scorpion series. However the presence of any military vehicles using tracks, rather than wheels would have given rise to accusations of the British bringing 'tanks' into Ulster, and this had to be avoided at all costs. (Henshaw Collection)

210. Saracens fitted with additional 'excrescence' against rocket attacks. (Henshaw Collection)

211. The Ferret two-man Scout Car has been widely used for reconnaissance and patrol duties by the British Army. (Henshaw Collection)

212. The ubiquitous Land Rover has appeared in many forms during the Ulster conflict. Many, like the vehicle pictured, are coated with GRP and Macralon plastic armour, resistant to bomb splinters and low-velocity small arms fire. (Henshaw Collection)

213. A Humber 'Pig' fitted with special equipment to launch a Wheelbarrow bomb-disposal device. (Henshaw Collection)

▲212　▼213

214. A rather special version of the Land Rover used by the RUC, with riot shields 'wings'. This version was used to drive into rioting crowds and virtually sweep them aside. Some minor damage, including missing digits from its number plate, indicates that this vehicle had been in action shortly before the picture was taken. (RUC)

215. The effects of an RPG-7 rocket attack on a RUC Land Rover coated with Macralon armour. The vehicle damage appears relatively light, but one officer was killed and another seriously injured in the incident on the outskirts of West Belfast. (RUC)

216. A Shorland light armoured car of the UDR taking part in a ceremonial parade in Belfast city centre. (Henshaw Collection)

▲214　▼215

▼216

217. A Saladin armoured car. This vehicle, based on the same six-wheel chassis as the Saracen, has only occasionally appeared in Ulster. It mounts a 76mm gun in a 360° rotating turret and is not really an appropriate vehicle to use in 'Aid to the Civil Power' situations. Some, without ammunition for the main armament, have been used, as command vehicles, the large turret giving protection and all-round visibility to the crew. Like the Saracen and the Ferret, this is an Alvis product with a Rolls-Royce engine. In the British Army it has been superseded for many years by tracked reconnaissance vehicles of the Scorpion family. Despite the size of its gun, equivalent to that of such battle tanks as the Sherman of the Second World War, it is NOT a *tank*, but an armoured reconnaissance vehicle. (Henshaw Collection)

218. A 'hybrid' Saracen/ Saladin mounting a new type of water cannon, capable of delivering short bursts of *very* high-pressure water, and possibly more effective than the earlier water cannon. (Henshaw Collections)

219. Another view of a Mk 3 Shorland light armoured car with smoke/CS gas dischargers and a visor for the commander. (Henshaw Collection)

▲217 ▼218

▼219

220. Although the main task for the RAF Wessex and Puma helicopters has been the movement of troops they can often help in other matters. A road-block being positioned on the Border in South Armagh. (Henshaw Collection)
221. A rather special task undertaken by Army Air Corps helicopters. This is a 'Heli-tele' Scout whcih can take moving-pictures from the air and simultaneously transmit the results to screens on the ground. (Henshaw Collection)
222. Helicopter crews always like to help the community when they can. A Royal Air Force Puma assisting in the rebuilding of an important spire in Derry. (Henshaw Collection)

220

▼221   222▶

223. 'Claribel' – a device enabling the crew of a patrol vehicle to identify instantly the direction from which fire is coming, and thereby respond to it. It is a miniature radar system which can be fitted into vehicles as small as a Land Rover. (Henshaw Collection)
224. 'Claribel' mounted in a Land Rover. (Henshaw Collection)
225. Buildings that started as Police Stations eventually became 'fortresses'. An armoured ambulance (Saracen) entering Hastings Street Police Station, Belfast in 1973. (Henshaw Collection)
226. The British Army fortress or 'sangar' in the front-lione Border town of Crossmaglen. (Henshaw Collection)

▲224 ▼225   226▶

▲227 ▼228

◀229 ▲230

▲231 ▼232

27. 'An Eagle VCP' – meaning a snap vehicle check-point near ¦e Border conducted by troops dropped quickly from an RAF ┆essex. (Henshaw Collection)

28. An Army Air Corps Scout helipcoper (on the ground) and an ₁F Puma (in the air) supplying a forward Army Border post. For ┆curity reasons the helicopter became a much safer means of ₁nsport then a land vehicle once the 'Border war' had been ┆ned. (Henshaw Collection)

29. 'Beehive' explosive charges being prepared for the cratering ┆ a Border road. (Henshaw Collection)

30. The imposition of delay upon the advance of enemy forces is ┆very ancient military art, going back to the spreading of nails or ┆arbles under horses' hooves. Numerous devices of this sort have ┆en used by the Security Forces (and their 'opposition') during ┆e Ulster Troubles. This device, consisting of a chain of ┆angulated spikes, one of which would always be upwards and ┆ould puncture a car tyre, is called a 'Caltrops'. The important ┆ing for a patrol to remember was to remove it before driving ┆vay themselves. This was sometimes forgotten, with ┆nbarrassing results. (Henshaw Collection)

31. 'Lazy Tongs', a lightweight version of 'Caltrops' introduced ┆about 1977. (Henshaw Collection)

32. 'Startrain', an even more sophisticated version of the 'nail'. ┆enshaw Collection)

Bomb disposal

▲233

▲234
◄235

233. An ATO (Ammunition Technical Officer) of the Royal Army Ordnance Corps donning his protective clothing. (Henshaw Collection)

234. An ATO dressed in the best possible protective clothing yet devised – body armour, helmet and visor, fireproof gloves and boots. Even this, however, will not ensure his life if something goes wrong with an explosive device at close quarters. (Henshaw Collection)

235. ATO with a typical suspicious object. (Henshaw Collection)

236. An ATO being 'dressed' before examining a suspected booby-trapped car. In the event this incident turned out to be a hoax, but the stresses and tensions are visible in the faces of all concerned. (Henshaw Collection)

237. ATO with a beer keg bomb. (Henshaw Collection)

▼238 ▲239

238. 'Wheelbarrow', the most important device ever invented for the extraction and disposal of bombs, and perhaps more importantly, for the preservation of the lives of ATOs. Earlier versions of Wheelbarrow were called 'Tortoise' or 'Little Willie', and later 'Goliath'. All were designed by inventive minds within the British Army, and owed something to techniques evolved by the flyers of radio-controlled model aeroplanes, and others who were happy to apply their knowledge of new technology in the micro-chip era to some of the Northern Ireland problems. (Henshaw Collection)

239. Wheelbarrow dealing with a hijacked lorry in South Armagh in 1975. (Henshaw Collection)

240. A Wheelbarrow descending the built-in ramps from an RAOC, or EOD (Explosive Ordnance Disposal) transit van. 'Transits' have been adopted as the best means of rapid transport for EOD teams for several years. (Henshaw Collection)

240

▲241

▲242 ▼243

241. Sometimes, however, EOD teams have had to move even faster, by air. An RAF Wessex drops a team and its equipment in South Armagh in 1975. (Henshaw Collection)

242. An RAF Puma helicopter landing a bomb-disposal (EOD) team near the Border. (Henshaw Collection)

243. A bomb-disposal team moves into an incident in South Armagh. The EOD Transit can be seen in the bottom left-hand corner of the picture with an Army Air Corps Scout giving protective cover overhead. An Army Land Rover is moving from right to left. Meanwhile Mr John Doyle's family washing hangs on the line and his little boat is on its trailer, perhaps ready for a fishing or water-skiing trip later in the day. (Henshaw Collection)

244. The incident continues. Two EOD Transits are in position with Land Rover cover 'fore and aft', and top-cover still provided by the Scout with a crewman-gunner at the ready in the starboard door. (Henshaw Collection)

244

▲245   ▼246

▲247

245, 246. Wheelbarrow being prepared for action. (Henshaw Collection)

247. Wheelbarrow looking at a potentially lethal Mini. This is probably a training picture in which this version of Wheelbarrow is described as a Mk 7. Another name for Wheelbarrow in its early days was 'Guided Grapnel' and it was once suggested that even more advanced versions might be called 'Marauders'. (Henshaw Collection)

248. An advanced (Mk 7) Wheelbarrow takes a look inside a tanker suspected of containing high explosives. (Henshaw Collection)

249. Wheelbarrow in action in Belfast with ATO, firemen, and a policeman. (Henshaw Collection)

248

249

250. An early version of Wheelbarrow, having punche[d] its way through the driver's window, takes a look at the interior of a suspect car. (Henshaw Collection)

251. This lorry, hijacked somewhere in the Irish Republic, had been loaded with about 600 pounds of explosives, in January 1980. A[ ]special Wheelbarrow had sawn out a section of the lorry's body by remote contro[l] enabling both the explosives and the '*Weetabix*' packets to[ ]be removed harmlessly. (Henshaw Collection)

252. RAOC bomb-disposal teams and others frequently had recourse to the 'controlle[d] explosion' technique to dispose of dangerous items. This car was believed to have been booby-trapped by the INLA. (Henshaw Collection)

▲250   ▼251

▼252

253. A Wheelbarrow with remote-control lead, approaching a suspect car, just visible round the corner. (Henshaw Collection)

254. Wheelbarrow was later given a 'Big Friend' – an armoured version of the fork-lift truck, nicknamed 'Eager Beaver'. This particular vehicle has in addition been affectionately named 'Mean Machine' by its crew, and bears the trophies of the outlines of eight car bombs painted below its 'cockpit', in the style adopted by Bomber Command during the Second World War. (The British Army has always tried to match the RAF in these matters. Many of its 'Green Goddess' fire-engines were similarly adorned with flame bursts and cats-up-trees when the Army helped out during the firemen's strike in the 1970s. (Henshaw Collection)

▲253   ▼254

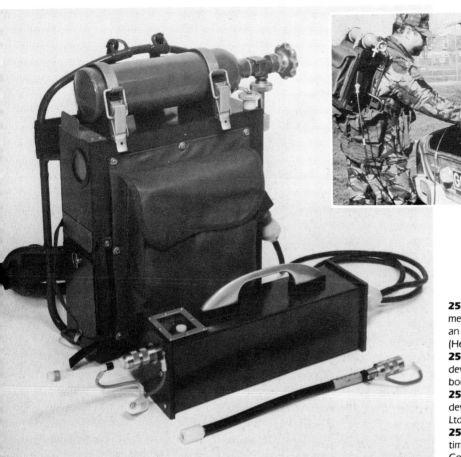

255. An advanced type of metal detector being used by an ATO of the RAOC. (Henshaw Collection)
256. An explosive 'sniffer' device being used on a car boot. (Henshaw Collection)
257. A metal detector developed by Pye Dynamics Ltd. (Henshaw Collection)
258. A typical IRA bomb-timing device. (Henshaw Collection)

255   ▲257   ▼258

Weapons of the IRA

▲259　▼260

259. A typical arms find. (RUC)
260. Arms find, Cambrai Street, Belfast in December 1981. Weapons include German Steyr rifles, an M.1 carbine, a Belgian FN, a handgun and a telescopic sight. (Henshaw Collection)
261. Another typical arms find. (RUC)
262. A 1979 haul including a US-made M.60 machine-gun and an RPG rocket launcher. (Henshaw Collection)

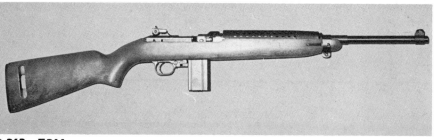

▲263 ▼264

263. The M.1 Carbine. A favourite IRA weapon and apparently readily available – at a price – on the world's arms markets. (RUC)

264. Home-made IRA hand-held grenade launchers found in 1985. (Henshaw Collection)

265. An RPG-7 rocket launcher with missile, capable of penetrating an armoured car. probably Soviet-designed, Czech-made. (Henshaw Collection)

266. And of a 'Heavy Browning' – a weapon used against low-flying aircraft during the Second World War and capable of downing a helicopter. (Henshaw Collection)

267. An IRA publicity picture of an M.60 machine-gun. (Henshaw Collection)

265

▲266   ▼267

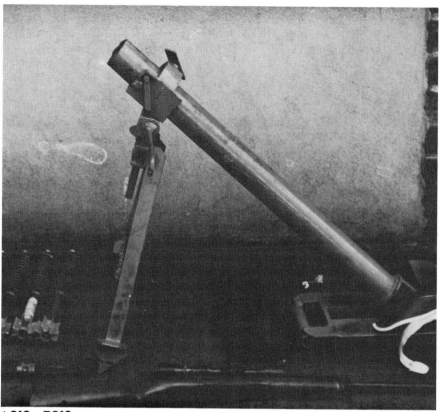

▲ 268 ▼ 269

268. Home-made mortar and bombs found in Lurgan in 1979. (Henshaw Collection)

269. A selection of IRA mortar bombs which have been classified into 'Marks' by the Security Forces. The smallest shown is a 'Mk 4', the largest a 'Mk 10'. (Henshaw Collection)

270. The aftermath of a 'thwarted' mortar attack in Newry in 1985. A sharp-eyed Traffic Warden spotted a youth running from a van and notified the Police. A wooden box with a switch marked 'Arm/Disarm' could be seen through the van windows. The area was evacuated and the van's contents were made safe by an ATO. They included four IRA home-made mortar tubes, pointing towards Newry Police Station. Picture shows the tubes and the explosive charges. Newry Police Station has been attacked on several occasions by mortars. (Henshaw Collection)

271. The Hitachi van concerned in the above episode. The tubes were mounted in the back, and a curtain was hung behind the front seats. The van roof had been removed and spray-painted cardboard substituted. (Henshaw Collection)

▲270 ▼271

272. IRA mortar tubes. Since the Chinese invention of gunpowder the 'mortar' has always been a relatively simple weapon to manufacture and use since it does not require precise machining nor the grooving of barrels as do rifles and artillery guns. Home-made mortars, however, are wildly inaccurate and their use is appallingly irresponsible; the innocent are just as likely to be killed or injured as the so-called 'hard targets'. This is exactly what has happened in a number of IRA mortar attacks. (Henshaw Collection, via RUC)

273. It became standard practice for the IRA to booby-trap the cabs of lorries used for mortar attacks. In turn, is now standard practice for ATOs to subject the cab to a controlled explosion before attempting to dismantle the weapons. (Henshaw Collection)

272

273

274. The damage done in the Station yard, showing the remains of the canteen which took a direct hit. (RUC)
275. The vehicle used in the IRA mortar attack on Newry Police Station, 28 February 1985, killing nine police officers. Note the use of innocent-looking wooden pallets to align the mortar tubes. (RUC)

274

275

276. Milk churn bombs, each containing about 100 pounds of explosives made from easily obtainable fertilizers and sugar. (Henshaw Collection)

277. A petrol bomb 'factory'. Note the petrol storage containers; milk bottles partly filled with sugar; measures and masks. (RUC)

278. Bombs under cars have taken the lives of many during the conflict, including that of Mr Airey Neave, MP, the Conservative spokesman on Northern Ireland, until his death outside the House of Commons in March 1979. This is a car bomb of the type which killed him, placed and 'claimed' by the INLA. (Henshaw Collection)

279. The Provisional IRA have tended to use cruder car bombs of the type illustrated here. (Henshaw Collection)

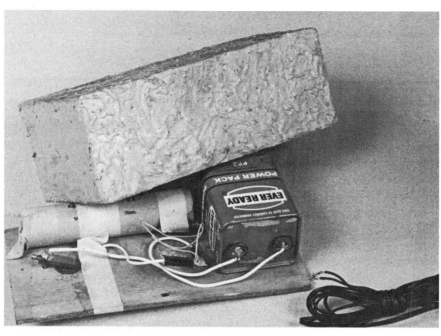

280. Bombs can take many guises. An ingenious IRA attempt to disguise one as an ornamental brick. (Henshaw Collection)
281. A miniature incendiary device employing a cheap wrist-watch and a tape-recorder casette-case. 'Cheap, simple, slips easily into the pocket,' the sales literature might say. Also deadly if it starts a fire in a crowded place. (Henshaw Collection)
282. A store of bombs, probably made from gas cylinders, found near Queen's University, Belfast. (Henshaw Collection)

280

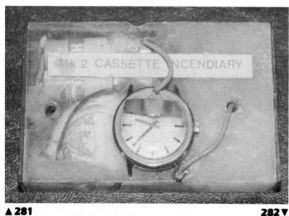

▲ **281**

282 ▼

283

283. A standard IRA bomb-timing unit, called 'Mk 15' by the Security Forces. Using easily obtainable parts such as the radio battery holder on the left and a kitchen oven timer, it can provide the necessary electrical power for a detonation with up to 60 minutes' delay. Far more sophisticated long-period timing devices have been used in recent years, but still employing equipment readily, and legally purchasable, such as the TV video-recorder, which can set up a programme, and equally, detonate a bomb, fourteen days ahead. (Henshaw Collection)

The Maze

▲ 284   285 ▶

284. The 'custom-built' prison to the south of Belfast, originally called Long Kesh, later The Maze, has of course become part of the folklore of the 'Irish Troubles'. An artist's impression, 'Long Kesh Dog Patrol' drawn in 1973. (Henshaw Collection)

285. A rare picture of prisoners inside The Maze, apparently taking part in a parade of Republican significance, perhaps a normal 'Muster Parade', with the Republican Colour flying. (Henshaw Collection)

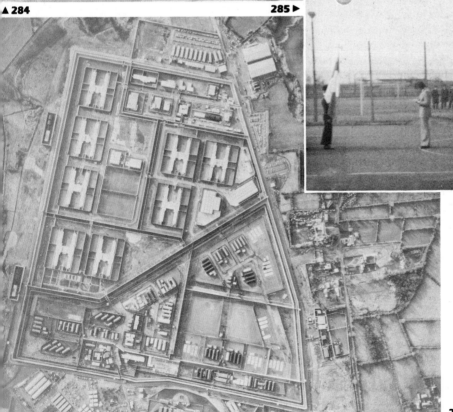

286. The cell blocks were built in the shape shown at the top of this aerial picture, hence the emergence of the evocative phrase 'H-Block'. (Henshaw Collection)

286

The Propaganda battle

DON'T LET THIS PUT YOU OUT OF BUSINESS

LIFE SIZE CASSETTE INCENDIARY

Most Incendiary devices are of the Cassette Ty,
But they can come in many shapes
They are often disguised by wrappings

Look for anything which feels odd:
Feels heavier or lighter or is out of place

Search your premises thoroughly and regularly
particularly after closing time

If you find one:

DO NOT TOUCH
EVACUATE THE AREA
INFORM THE POLICE - DIAL 999

Issued by the RUC

▲ 289

290 ▶

MURDER MURDER
MURDER MURDER MURDER MURDER

This is what the bombers did

to a human being

MURDER MURDER MURDER MURDE

MURDER MURDER MURDER MURD

MURDER MURDER

293, 294 (overleaf).
Security warnings on the mainland.

Note: all illustrations in this section of the
book from the Henshaw Collection.

*The 1st Battalion The Royal Green Jackets
invite you
to help stop terrorism in Belfast
It's in your interest to report
anything suspicious
Phone Belfast 25677 or 24421*

291

1st BATTALION
THE ROYAL GREEN JACKETS
North Queen Street · Belfast 26332
Thank you for your co-operation.
We regret any delay or inconvenience but
YOUR SAFETY IS OUR CONCERN

287. A UDR recruiting poster.
288. A Security Forces warning.
289. RUC appeal to businessmen.
290. Security Forces appeal for help after a bombing in which twelve people were killed.
291, 292. Royal Greenjackets 'Public Relations'.

292

TERRORIST ALERT

26 MAR 74, CLARO-DEVERELL BARRACKS, RIPON

PRINCESS LOUISE'S KENSINGTON REGIMENT

2 DEC 80 – TA CENTRE, HAMMERSMITH

12 FEB 76, NATIONAL DEFENCE COLLEGE, LATIMER

REGULAR OR TA, URBAN OR RURAL, ALL ARE TARGETS TO THE TERRORIST

Photographs courtesy of Press Association

PUBLISHED BY 9 SY COY

TERRORIST ALERT

REGENTS PARK 20 JUL 82.
7 MEMBERS OF 1 RGJ BAND KILLED AND 27 PEOPLE INJURED

WHENEVER YOUR BAND IS TO PLAY IN PUBLIC YOU ARE REQUIRED TO NOTIFY THE LOCAL ARMY DISTRICT HEADQUARTERS

(Army Bands: See AGAI Issue 52 paras 8. 071–8.076)

Photographs courtesy of Press Association

Published by HQ UKLF G2 Sy

294

Irish
Republican
Army-1981

295

Victory
to those strugglin
for Ireland's freedom

IRA
IN ACTION
1982

296

IRA
1983

"We mean to be free, and
in every enemy of tyranny
we recognise a brother,
wherever he takes his
place, in every land where
freedom lives. We recog-
nise our enemy, though
he were as Irish as our
hills.
"The whole of Ireland
for the people of Ireland
— their public property
to be owned and operat-
ed as a national heritage
by the labour of the men
in a free country.
"That is our idea, and
when you ask us what are
our methods, we reply:
'Those which lie nearest
our hands.'"
— James Connolly

297

298

299

IRISHMEN and IRISHWOMEN

DON'T BELIEVE ANY RUMOURS

Republican aims are still the same . . . . .

ENGLAND OUT— AND AN ALL-IRELAND REPUBLIC

THERE WILL BE NO COMPROMISE WITH REPUBLICAN PRINCIPLES !

ISSUED BY OGLAIGH NA hEIREANN

300

301

02

303

304

Update

Hopes and fears continued to see-saw through Spring and summer of 1986.

In April the Protestant reaction against the Anglo-Irish Agreement reached unexpected proportions of violence, with serious rioting in Portadown following a ban placed on a proposed Protestant Apprentice Boys march. A few days later, an extraordinary series of attacks by Protestant extremists against the Royal Ulster Constabulary began. They took the form of the petrol-bombing of policemen's homes, threats to their wives and children and direct assaults on officers. This seemed to be a total 180-degree reversal of the attitudes taken during the early days of 'The Troubles' when the RUC was so often accused of being 'on the Protestant side'.

Although British Regular Army casualties remained light in comparison with those of the '70s, there were some grievous incidents, including the death of a young Royal Greenjacket only hours after his arrival in the Province on his first tour of duty, and that of a distinguished officer of the Royal Anglian Regiment, Major Andrew French. By May 1986 the total death toll in the six months since the signing of the Anglo-Irish Agreement had reached 26. In June the Northern Ireland Secretary, Mr. Tom King, had to announce the dissolution – at least temporarily – of the Northern Ireland Assembly because of the Unionist stance, thus taking the clock back by four years to a resumption of direct rule from Westminster.

On the industrial front there was also good news and bad. Shorts signed an agreement with Boeing to build a substantial proportion of the parts for the revolutionar 7J7 propfan airliner due to enter service in 1992. It wa estimated that the deal would create 1,000 new jobs an be worth some £200 million. Amongst some controvers and bitterness on the mainland, Harland & Wolff won battle against Swan Hunter of Tyneside to build the first a fleet of six new Royal Fleet Auxiliary supply ships at price of £130 million. The bad news included the closure the Rothman cigarette plant at Carrickfergus with the lo of nearly 800 jobs, and an announcement by the Gener Electricity Company of more redundancies. The overa unemployment rate stood at a depressing 21.4%.

Outside the Province, major events included the extra ordinary blunder over the release from custody in Dubli of the IRA bombing suspect Evelyn Glenholmes and, on different note, the result of the trial of the Brighton hot bomber Patrick Magee, together with others accused planning a 'carnage' campaign on the mainland. Th conclusion of the trial enabled newspapers to reveal th extraordinary skills and patience used by the police t track down and capture the accused.

Negotiations for more satisfactory extradition arrange ments in the United States tended to ebb and flo between frustration and success, but the British natio was left with the feeling that too many American 'cousin remain uninformed about what is really involved.

Again, the final comment can only be that there is n room for complacency, but that there are still man grounds for hope.

J.C. (23 June 1986

105. The result of Protestant extremist petrol-bombing at an RUC reservist's house off the Shankill Road. (*Belfast Telegraph*)

306. 25 June 1986: a month before their wedding, Prince Andrew and Miss Sarah Ferguson delighted Belfast people by paying a surprise visit to the city. (*Belfast Telegraph*)

ACKNOWLEDGEMENTS

The compiler would like to thank the authors and publishers of the following books for the information contained in them which provided vital checks against his own memories and records:

CALLAGHAN, Rt.Hon. L. James. *A House Divided.* Collins, 1973.

DEWAR, Lieutenant-Colonel Michael. *The British Army in Northern Ireland.* Arms & Armour Press, 1985.

FLACKES, W. D. *Northern Ireland; A Political Diary.* Ariel Books/BBC, 1980.

HAMILL, Desmond. *Pig in the Middle.* Methuen, 1985.

KEE, Robert. *Ireland, A History.* Weidenfeld & Nicholson, 1980.

STYLES, George, GC. *Bombs Have No Pity.* William Luscombe, 1975.

He would also like to thank many of his 'fellow-hacks' and old friends in the profession of journalism (sometimes called 'The Inky Trade') for their help in trying to get this record right. We had many adventures together, some of which we might prefer to forget, yet I hope we may all be able to take some pride in this book.
        J.C